For Mama and Papka.

Chapter I

I'm three years old, and I'm riding my old, green, frequently repaired tricycle, in a cobbled yard of the house I grew up in. It is the first memory I conjure up when I think of the provenance of my existence in this world. How peculiar that everything was already here before I could remember anything: people I knew already lived here and did things, discussed politics and the lives of others, global events took place, our house stood in the same place as it did now, my family members argued and disliked each other, and nobody had any knowledge of me. Then suddenly, I was pedalling my tricycle, and now I was also part of all this, but before, I was sound asleep in some dark, sealed box. Then somebody woke me up and gave me a role to play along with those who had woken up before me. I had become relevant. I was a human.

Naturally, these weren't the thoughts I had at the time, of course not. I had no thoughts, I just felt happy.

I don't know why I think my tricycle had been broken and fixed before. Since it was old, it must have belonged to other children first.

My Mama procured it from somewhere, and I rode it until I was too big for it. But until then, I was three, and I was riding in our yard on a sunny summer's day, surrounded by our neighbours, my friends and family members. My family consisted of my brother Felix, my sisters, Varvara and Jelena, our Mama and Papka, and me. There was also a cat, Vasily and a mongrel, Rubik. We lived in a one-bedroom flat in a tenement house. There were seven more flats occupied by former and present teachers. Papka was an English teacher and that is why we lived there - in the elite house of the village. Our very understanding, generous, and impatient neighbours didn't really like us. That was because all their children had grown up and moved to the big cities to raise their grandchildren, allowing them to enjoy peace and quiet. And because they all had teaching jobs at the village school and no mouths to feed, they didn't have the need to keep livestock, plough fields and harvest the hay. They frowned upon our rubber farm boots, and our smelly bucket with food leftovers for our pigs, outside our flat door. We were very grateful for their contribution of leftovers to the bucket, and to show this gratitude the first thing that Mama told me to do when we slaughtered a pig, was to take some fresh pork to our neighbours. I could see their faces light up when they looked at that mince and ribs, and my face lit up too, when I turned to go and I heard; "Nastassja, wait, take some sweets please". There were sweets for me at home, but they were the cheapest kind. Teachers always had the best sweets saved for moments like this. Being invited to come inside their child-free homes was always alluring to me. Some were more likely to invite me in than others: the ones whose sons and daughters hadn't given them grandchildren of a similar age to me, almost never asked me to come inside. I too had my preferences based on the household smells.

Whenever I left someone's home, I wondered what our smell was and why I couldn't smell it. Did these people know that I would be able to tell whose house I was in with a blindfold on if I had to?

The house residents took pride in keeping the outside area green, lush with wild cherry trees, bushes and flower beds. A real oasis of tranquillity if it wasn't for our imperative need to graze little chicks, goslings, and ducklings in the spring and early summer weeks. Once they became bigger, they were taken to the barn, where they laid eggs and got killed for meat, either by us or some vile, nocturnal animals, such as massive rats. I felt sad when I heard what happened when I wasn't there to protect them anymore. Grazing those baby birds was my first serious responsibility. Mama and Felix would get up early to drive to the farm market to get the piglets and birdies. A cheeky baby pig once extricated itself from a sack and spread out comfortably on the back seat of the car like a goddess.

"Mama, please don't freak out, just look calmly in the front mirror." said my brother, who was driving. Quite the view that must have been.

By the time I was out of bed, the box with the tiniest, softest, warmest, gaggling, toy-like offspring would be waiting for me. I was tasked with taking their box out every morning and placing them in a wooden bottomless frame, capped with a wire spring cover to prevent cats getting inside. I had to ensure there was food and water available for them throughout the day. In the evening, I counted them and moved them back to the box for the night. One morning, we found Vasily sleeping comfortably on top of the chicks. Not only did he not crush them, but he also kept everyone warm and snug. Vaska was never a threat to his own, but frogs and mice had to watch out for him.

When the birds were two weeks old, I would let them out of the frame but never out of my sight. That was what really exasperated our respectable neighbours: having to put up with the smell of my flock's droppings beneath their windows, which they felt ruined the view of the elite house. Yet, what my teacher-neighbours detested about us the most was me.

I was a child like any other, with a healthy amount of energy and spirit and an occasional penchant for mischief, thanks to my impressionable nature and the influences of the other children. The stuffy house community hated all the qualities that children possess, and hence intimidated me and those who came by to play with me. The house was situated among a few other blocks of flats, but they all looked so characterless and stark compared to ours. My Mama used to say the flats in those houses were designed better, and had more space and bigger kitchens. Our house was the oldest communist block in our village and while they were building it, angst-ridden youth would come round at night and knock some of the bricks down. So I heard from none other than my mama. Our family friend, Mr Luktuk, told her because he had been one of those teenagers.

All my playmates came from those blocks. I had outgrown my tricycle by then and my best friend at this time was Evie.

Despite being twins, Evie and Princess bore no resemblance to each other in appearance or temperament. Evie was transparent and slow, while Princess was dominant and focused. Their mother dressed them in the same clothes and wouldn't let them out of the house in winter, only to school and back. Apparently, they couldn't afford winter clothes and boots. There was also Greta – a cunning, calculating, and cruel girl, who was a friend and a bully. Greta was our family friends' daughter. Her older sisters were friends with Varvara and Felix, our mothers were close friends. We also shared the same cattle shed and cow pastures. Greta's family was always better off than mine. The Leach girls had the trendiest clothes, bikes, a videotape player, a colour TV, a Hi-Fi, portable radio, and cassette player.

They also had considerable latitude to go anywhere they liked and come back home any time they chose. Because the flats were better where the Leaches lived, they had hot water and very efficient heating at home. We didn't, and sometimes, they were kind enough to allow us to have a hot wash at their place.

When money was tight for us, which was pretty much all the time, Mama would pour out some of their shampoo and washing powder to take back with us. If they did notice it, they never gossiped about that. Not to give the impression that in between those rare moments when we went to the Leaches, we maintained low levels of hygiene, I must describe the bathing system in our household. There was no central heating and no boilers in our elite house. In every flat there was a tiled stove powered by logs. It'd serve as a cooking stove and give warmth to the rooms via tiled walls. Every evening we'd boil a massive steel pot of hot water and share it among ourselves by taking turns in the bathtub. I'd be helped by my oldest and kindest sibling, Jelena. She'd wash my hair while I covered my eyes with a towel for fear of water getting in my eyes.

Jelena reused the water after me to wash her long, luxuriant locks.

Girls in the neighbourhood nicknamed Greta *Leech* - a petty response to her treating us superciliously, just because her family had more money. Greta had a doll-like face and naturally curly hair. Mama and Jelena liked complimenting her attractive demeanour in front of me. Jelena plaited my hair into French braids every day, tantalizing me with the prospect of having curly hair 'just like Greta's'. Luckily for me, Greta grew out of her baby doll appearance by the age of ten, and nobody thought she was a doll anymore. There was also a ginger-haired girl, Ausra, who was half-witted and only hung out with younger children. When Ausra was in her mid-teens, she thought it was very funny to pour a bucket of cold water over her sleeping uncle.

"Gingers are not people! I never understood why your mother kept you!" roared Ausra's startled uncle.

Another older girl, Laura, occasionally dropped into our games, but really she just wanted to cause intrigue and spread gossip. Both Laura's parents were chronic alcoholics, who used to make their children run errands late in the evening for them. Laura was a cruel child, for only a cruel child would create a wedge between her parents and laugh when her father beat her mother and stepbrother.

In summer, from morning to evening, it was impossible to get me home: Greta Leach, the twins and I would play French skipping, hopscotch, hide and seek, running and chasing games. I must have been the most gullible out of us all. In spite of my weak physical ability to compete with them at French skipping, and my obvious preference for playing a game which I was better at, my selfish friends convinced me to hold the elastic for them throughout the whole game. I had weak legs and couldn't jump higher than knee level, thus mostly I just 'stood inside the elastic'.

My favourite game was playing out simple, domestic scenarios of the imagined adult-motherhood life. We needed very little to create the setting of the home, mainly playing with 'air objects' and describing them to one another. I remember one time I was playing in Greta Leach's flat, where we were both housewives, helplessly imitating our own mothers. Greta told me that her imaginary children were playing outside right now, and she was alone with her imaginary husband. Then she asked me if I wanted to see what she and her husband were doing.

I said; "Sure."

Greta went into her parents' bedroom, lay on her front on their bed, with both her arms tucked underneath her while thrusting her hips backwards and forwards. She let out short, low grunts and said; "This is what we're doing."

"Why?" I asked.

"We're making more children," she answered.

Greta was the most self-serving girl I'd known. She was two years my senior but already had a rapacious and cunning streak in her. When I grew older, I realised that she only hung out with me when there was no one better around, or when she needed something from me. Mrs. Leach allowed her daughters to bring friends, and later, boyfriends home, unlike my Mama. Out of all my local friends, only Greta Leach was permitted to come inside our home. My Mama never seemed to have an issue with our friendship, even though she could also see that I was being used and sometimes abused by the girl. We were once again at the Leaches, when I really wanted to go outside and play, but my friend insisted that I must massage her soles first. I told her I didn't want to do it, but she convinced me that we were in one of her imaginary situations now where she couldn't step on her feet because of the big, evil bees inside them, and only I could help her to get rid of them. Being foolish and impressionable, I yielded to all her terms. I massaged and tickled both her soles while she kept apprising me of the progress of the bees.

"It's helping, I can tell it's helping, they have now been disturbed so they are beginning to leave," she explained.

"Greta, are they still inside?" I asked after a few more moments.

"Almost. It's the queen bee that I'm worried about," she said; "She is the hard one to get rid of. Just keep tickling my heels now as I think she's there."

"What about now, Greta, has she gone now?" I was starting to get rather tired and impatient now.

"Just a little more. I'll tell you when she's out." I was overcome with uncomfortable sadness and told her I was going home. Greta jumped to her feet instantly and assured me that she'd been cured thanks to me.

Mr Leach bought his daughters a trendy, so-called 'sports bike' with gears. Every teenager of that time coveted one, but only a few could own one. The Leaches had several different bikes: the 'female bike' due to the absence of crossbar, the 'male bike' with a crossbar and the 'sports bike' with gears. In our household there was only one bike with a crossbar. It was the same colour as my tricycle and was prone to breaking. Our Papka didn't know how to fix it, but he excelled at cursing it every time it broke. He cursed things in and out of his control. Once while we were outside, the rain started pouring down on us and he became irate.

"Devil take it! Curse this weather! Curse this rain! Devil take it!" I felt frightened and wanted Mama. It was the very first time I had heard such powerful curses.

Luckily, there were other people who could fix bikes for a small fee when the gear chain fell off, or some other defect plagued our bike. The cows in the pastures two miles away had to be attended to and milked without fail, come rain or shine, so Mama would have to hang the milk buckets on the bike handles and push it in front of her.

Greta loved showing off her new bicycle and so one day she asked me if I wanted to ride with her. Being a fledging cyclist, I couldn't believe what a joyous experience I was about to have...up until then I had only ridden our old, clunky bike, with one leg thrust underneath the frame to reach the pedal on the other side, with my head barely at the height of the handles. We all learned to cycle with these old, heavy, Soviet bikes and we all cried with pain when we hit our groins with it. I knew well that the front wheel might come off, as one time when Mama took me with her to the pastures, it had happened. I was perching on the crossbar and we were going downhill when it fell off. I heard myself screaming at the top of my voice, and this woman came rushing to our aid. She told me off for yelling.

"Will you stop howling, for the love of God?" The woman scooped my shocked Mama off the road. "Nearly missed it." She said "Stop screaming, you're all right, have some compassion for your poor mother!" I didn't know what I'd done wrong and raised my voice to get some sympathy. I was terrified by what had just happened and scared of that woman shaming me. Mama didn't say anything at first, then she started to cry. Why was that woman so hostile towards me? I had just fallen off the bike too.

Bless my little pure heart - Greta didn't bestow the honour on me of even touching her new two-wheeler, nor did she offer me a lift on the back rack that every bike owner used as a passenger seat. Oh no. No, not Greta Leach. That wicked girl made me run alongside her while she raced her shiny fast bike, easily overtaking me. Even after such a strenuous effort on my part, I still hoped to have a go at it until my Mama saw me from our balcony and called me home immediately.

My brief friendship with Greta gradually waned. She struck up a friendship with Princess, whereas I became closer to her sister. My new best friend was a kind and gentle girl. One of the best things she ever did for me was to construct a house out of heavy-duty plastic sheets. She propped it up with tree branches and pinned it together with little spruce needles. Everyone was jealous of this magnificent construction and flooded in to gawk at it; and my pride in having it built in my yard for me was through the roof. This also meant I could exert my power over who I wanted to play with us. Evie also created such a lovely interior design, that even my neighbours admired her skill and craftsmanship. Our rocky comradeship ended abruptly one day when she put her foot down and decided not to endure any more physical abuse from me. The house she built was the highest indication of our steadfast friendship, so to punish me she took it all apart in front of me. I deserved to be dumped for my frequent bouts of violence, which manifested in an uncontrollable urge to purse my lips and kick Evie in the leg. The early, abusive streaks of my child personality were triggered by as little as childish jealousy and the need to take it out on someone or something. With Evie, I didn't even need a reason to inflict pain on her. I once kicked her on the shin just because I felt like it. There was something comforting about the way she handled me, which assured me she'd never leave. I was strongly attached to my benign friend, so when she started unpinning the needles from the polyester sheets and refused to forgive me, I felt broken-hearted and betrayed, but I was as yet unable to identify those feelings.

Besides these companions, I also had two summer and Christmas holiday friends. My super tall friend, Irmantas, who happened to be a boy, was one year my senior and had a funny accent. His overbearing, short-tempered grandmother was a primary school teacher with a menacing air about her. She was opposed to children playing with me in our outdoor area, and only encouraged us to do so when Irmantas was staying with her. Ona was kind, but her wrath was a gatekeeper to that kindness. When mama asked her to lend us some money, or when my siblings knocked on her door for some bread - this was from the times I couldn't recall because I was still sleeping in a dark box - first, they had to endure being harangued by Ona with her bitter litany of complaints: we were a bunch of impoverished beggars, incapable of earning the money ourselves and having to impose on her. How did we think she earned her living? She was retired but she was still working, and she was poor herself, she had a starving son in the city whose family depended on her wages and her pension. My parents shouldn't have had that many children if they were struggling to support them. She didn't have any money, we were mistaken. At the end of this impulsive speech, she'd pull out her purse and hand my mama a note or bread from the cupboard for my sister.

During the Christmas holidays, I'd spend most days with Irmantas playing in his grandmother's kitchen. The kitchen table was sticky with the leftovers of food, so Irmantas had to give it a good wipe before we could play on it. How we enjoyed each other's company! We were always on the same wavelength and had an equally rich imagination. Time would fly by when we were together.

Ona fed us Belgian waffles or crepes with a sweet filling every day. Whenever school started and Irmantas had to go back to the city, I would ask mama to make me Belgian waffles like Irmantas's grandmother. I would feel overwhelmed with nostalgic memories of those blissful moments. The only thing was that we didn't have a Belgian waffle maker, so I had to ask either my friend's granny or a rather peculiar couple downstairs to lend us one. That peculiar couple were both teachers with strong convictions, bordering on chauvinism. They also had a young niece, Rasa, who just like Irmantas, visited her uncle and aunt and spent all her holidays in the country. Rasa was about three years my junior, pampered by her overprotective relatives who were certain of her impeccability. You could always tell these city kids apart: only they would wear socks with sandals and they had clean, unbruised arms and legs. They'd also be afraid of climbing trees and falling out of them. They'd have to be home by dusk, not wander outside the permitted area and not mix with certain types of children. I wanted to wear socks with sandals too, but I was a village girl. It would have been ridiculous if I had.

There were times, however, when both my village and city friends played together. My teacher-neighbours never expressed their discontent at these times. The TV series *Baywatch* was our favourite game to emulate. Irmantas always got to play Mitch Buchannon, as he was the only boy, and all the girls wanted to play C J Parker. It was explained to me that I couldn't be her because she was blond, and I didn't even look like a Lithuanian.

There weren't any Asian-looking actresses in the show, so I was given the part of Stephanie, Mitch's girlfriend. No one thought she was pretty since she was brunette. I didn't think so either, but I had to work with what was available. Another reason I detested playing Stephanie was that everyone kept teasing Irmantas and me, saying we were a couple. His parents called me their daughter-in-law. The older generation, Felix and Varvara's associates, thought we looked very cute together playing a married couple in everyday, mundane scenarios, such as driving a car to the market to sell our homegrown apples. Irmantas once gave me his mother's discarded purses. We kids all liked to play with the stuff that our parents didn't need anymore. Such items were multi-functional and could be reused in many different games. When I told mama about my precious gifts, the innocent rumour swiftly spread that Irmantas was courting me. A weird sensation of disgust and shame filled me inside.

Children are known for their callousness to one another, partially shaped by what their parents talk about in their presence, and the prime example of this was Brigita's family. Brigita's father was a severely blind alcoholic, although his night vision was superb when it came to thieving from his neighbours. They had many children like my own family, except they were happy to live on welfare instead of working for their own bread by doing what everyone else did - agriculture. Brigita lived in unhygienic conditions and bore the appearance of an unkempt, smelly child. The first time I set foot in her place, I was appalled by the residue of wallpaper hanging off the walls, the dirty curtains, and the clothes scattered on the floor. Mama forbade me to go to Brigita's or to maintain the friendship altogether, even though she was the one who, out of pity, introduced her to us. No one wanted to be friends with Brigita and her siblings. We all steered away from her and called her mean names, mainly pertaining to her father's inclination to dress as a woman. We'd call her 'the transvestite's daughter' but in much more derogatory terminology, without knowing the meaning of such words. She would come around to my yard and sit just outside it watching us play. We refused outright to include her in our games and tried to make her go away by calling her names, but she'd just sit there unmoved and continue watching us as if she was looking at the TV screen. In one of those instances, Mama was passing by and upon witnessing such unfairness, she admonished us for our conduct towards Brigita and ordered us to include her. And so we did.

Chapter II

Cruelty is not a trait reserved solely to children. The latest, juiciest gossip bonds people in the oddest circumstances. The part of my flawed human essence which responds to such things was triggered for the first time when Regina was brutally murdered. The details of the gruesome murder were the hot topic for a while in my village. The story was even covered in the newspaper Mama subscribed to, called *Confrontation*. Regina was a single mother with learning disabilities, who lived alone and harboured a dream of bringing her little girl back home. She saved up from her monthly disability payments to buy clothes and toys for her daughter. The police found the killers who were from another village in the neighborhood and were known to Regina, which was why she opened her door to them in the middle of the night. The two men raped and killed her by stabbing her thirteen times with a fork. The old couple next door claimed not to have heard a thing, but people said they were just too scared to get involved. Everyone was talking about it and so I overheard this story time and again from everyone: Jelena, Mama, our neighbours talking among themselves.

Confrontation was a weekly newspaper that only covered police investigations of criminal cases. Our next-door neighbour, Vytas, a retired teacher, sacked from school for his little love for a drink, openly expressed his indignation if anyone but he laid his hands on a fresh copy of the newspaper first. There must have been only two avid readers of such contents in the entire village - my Mama and Vytas. Vytas liked the idea of co-owning our pets too; the mongrel, Rubik, chained to the kennel outside our house, was an excellent guide dog if you got lost in the woods, and as a mushroom and foraging enthusiast, Vytas often did. Our cat would disappear for days on end sometimes. Mama said he was visiting his female friends. One cold winter, we all accepted his overlong disappearance as a definite case of unexpected death. Everyone always told me to stop hassling the cat because he was old. He'd been old since I was little. Vasily came back two weeks later with frozen ear tips that later fell off and never grew back. It turned out Vytas had unintentionally locked him up in his garage in the low temperatures of winter. The chauvinist neighbour downstairs asked my Mama why she had clipped Vaska's ears. Mama found his question offensive. I was there when baby Vaska was brought home by Felix. He hid underneath Mama's bed, which she shared with Jelena and balked at any human contact. Felix and I bickered about which one of us was going to sleep with him, disregarding Mama's strict instructions to let the cat out for the night.

Felix always felt cold at night and slept underneath a tall pile of duvets and liked to snuggle up to the cat too. Come to think of it now, Vasily preferred sleeping with my brother to me. Whenever I grabbed him first, he always tried to escape. When my grip over him relaxed, he was quick to move. Mama would come around the living room – turned into a bedroom at night, which in later years I shared with my brother - and ask if I had a cat with me.

"No," was always my answer.

Then she'd remind me that someone would have to get up to let him out in the middle of the night or else he would do his business by the door. I would give a truthful answer the second time.

During the day, Vasily would make many trips in and out of the flat. He would stand by the door and meow asking to be let out, then five minutes later he would do the same on the other side of the door. This was the most annoying trait about him. But this was not why I used to hit him on the head and then kiss and stroke him afterwards. I liked seeing his little ears bend back in anticipation of the strike. Felix told me once that cats land on their feet and that they truly have nine lives. To check this theory, I threw Vasya down three flight of stairs. I wasn't quite satisfied with his landing, so I caught him and threw him once more. He did land on all fours neatly the second time. Vasya loved me despite all those horrid things I did to him. I know he is watching me from cat heaven. I loved squeezing him tight, except when he shed.

"Nastassja, put the cat down, can't you see its fur is crumbling!" Mama's vivid description of our cat's hair dispersion on anything it touched, became a running joke in our family. Ten times a day I had to sweep his shedding fur, but I never minded it. I loved sweeping and often our neighbours saw me singing and sweeping our staircase.

Most of our neighbours were benevolent to Rubik and Vasya. Rubik was given bones and the leftovers of soup, Vasya received a lot of petting and bits and pieces of fish and meat, although he had a cheek to sneak inside their flats and help himself. I think he disliked some other neighbours downstairs because frequently he'd leave them a present outside their door.

"Your cat has defecated on my door mat again!" A neighbour downstairs, another primary school teacher and former friend of Mama's yelled. Before I was born, my family moved here with the best furniture at the time and genuine wool carpets, thanks to Mama's dowry. Everyone wanted to be their friends, but after I was born, the times changed dramatically, and my family was no longer perceived as being good enough to socialize with the village schoolteachers. I never saw my birth as a starting point for my family's reduced circumstances.

"I am sorry, I will clean it right away," said Mama coming back from the evening cow-milking chores.

"It's dreadful!" the neighbour insisted.

"It's not dreadful. It's unpleasant, I understand, and we will clean it right away, but it's not dreadful. I'll tell you what was dreadful. When I carried that illegal medication through the Russian-Lithuanian border for your sick granddaughter, fully aware of the consequences had I got caught. Believe me, that was dreadful." Mama reminded her of the perilous favour she had delivered out of the kindness of her heart. The neighbour had no comeback to this because her granddaughter had been cured with this banned Russian medication.

People were always weird to us.

Throughout my childhood and teenage years, I was conscious of someone making racist remarks to me or my family members. I tried not to be in the places where it was most likely to happen or to pass by people who tended to make such comments, but more often than not , I had no choice. At a very young age I couldn't fathom out why I was singled out for supposedly looking different. I couldn't see that I looked any different to anyone else where I lived. The subsequent realisation came to me as I grew up.

Everything about my family seemed different in a tiny community in the backwaters of the country.

I must have been four or five at this point when Jelena took me to the church on Palm Sunday. We weren't Catholics and we weren't even baptized in any faith yet.

Jelena took me everywhere with her. We went to the event, and I joined the queue with the others and watched this priest handing out little bags of sweets and mini psalm books. I waited, he approached, and he skipped me. One time, my sister was getting her ends trimmed at the only barber-hairdresser's place in our village, when a hairstylist began bad-mouthing our priest while he sat outside and listened to how she thought he could improve his personality and his parish services. Everyone else waiting listened with him. He was her next customer. The bewildered woman said she didn't know he was sitting outside. I wondered which one of them felt more embarrassed.

My lovely Jelena was a talented knitter. She ensured that everyone in the family had enough winter socks, mittens, and jumpers. It was her favourite downtime activity besides playing the piano, studying, weeding and watering our vegetables in the summer months and crocheting cute tablecloths.

Jelena had excellent grades at school and dreamed of getting a free place in the medical university. A free place was her only option. Our neighbour, a biology and chemistry teacher, agreed to tutor her after lessons. What payment arrangements she and Mama had agreed to, I do not know.

Whenever my sister knitted something for me, she needed me to stay still for a few moments while she checked if the garment still matched my measurements. It was only a few moments that I had to oblige her, but to me they seemed like an eternity, especially if I had my friends waiting for me outside. Sometimes I felt as if Jelena didn't want me to socialise with them, as if she was a little too protective of me. She would be incensed whenever I let my hair loose just like the rest of the girls did. No one plaited their hair at home, their parents didn't care much for French plaits, but Jelena would drag me home and do my hair again. I couldn't understand why she was so angry with me. I just wanted to look pretty, and you don't look pretty with your hair done like that.

We had a piano at home, but only Jelena was sufficiently skilled to play a full range of keys. Both of my sisters went to the musical school; however, Varvara didn't show enough passion and later Mama couldn't afford to pay for her to continue. I kept asking my Mama why I couldn't play.

"You didn't go to school to learn to play," she would say.

"Why didn't I go, Mama?" I wanted to know.

"Well," she'd say "after you were born, life changed. There wasn't any spare money to pay for the school, and no means of transport to travel there."

"But can't I go now? I want to play this piano, like Jelena", I hoped to still have an option, and tried reasoning. "It can't be too late for me to start." When I grew a little older and brought the subject up again, Mama would conclude.

"Feeding you was a priority; I'd be cooking your pasta and have to look away to keep my own hunger at bay." Even though I could never play it, it didn't matter as much anymore. No one else had a piano at home and that sufficed. In those rare, harmonious family moments when my sisters and my mama would gather around the piano to sing to Jelena's playing, she'd sight-read from the music notes. *Yesterday* by *The Beatles* and *Silent Night* (even in summer) were among our favourite songs. Varvara would have a go at some easy tunes too. I always thought that all she lacked was a little tenacity to fulfill her potential, and nothing else.

From June to early August, everyone in the neighbourhood would cool themselves down by the local river. It was a real blessing to have the river on our doorstep. I wasn't allowed to go there without the supervision of an adult, unlike the rest of the children who enjoyed this prerogative. The good thing was,

Varvara and Felix could always be found there. Those two belonged to a group of friends called *The Rock Gang*, which consisted of around twenty members of their local and city friends. Past sunset, they'd all gather around a massive rock opposite our house and annoy the residents with their raucous noise. Eager to rush back to their friends first thing in the afternoon, Felix and Varvara would finish their house and farm chores in the morning, before slinking away to the hormone-driven action hub. The teenage boys chased and threw clothed girls into the water, in such a way as to display their physical attraction. The older Leach girls were the only ones with a portable cassette-radio player, powered on huge cylinder-shaped batteries that ran out very quickly. Couples for a balmy season formed and parted there. My brother had supplanted the crucial male figure in our family from a very young age. This came with many responsibilities, most being hard physical labour. Mama would send me to find Felix to remind him to give water to the cows in the afternoon or to do some other manly tasks. Felix never refused. All I needed to do was stand at the top of the hill and yell; "Felix!"

"What?!" sometimes would come as a response, but mostly I'd just rest my case all in one shriek.

"Felix! Mama told you to go to see to the cows! Now!" Splashing in the shallow bank of the river was also one of my favourite, but not very frequent, pastimes. Jelena had very little in common with her younger siblings or anyone else in the village. She relished tranquil solo swims at the other, less popular end of the river. I didn't appreciate being taken there. It was too deep and too cold for me, and there was no promenade for me to jump from. To add to my horrors, I couldn't escape from the thought of Jelena's classmate who had drowned there. I imagined him dragging me down to the bottom of the river, even though I had seen his body dressed in a suit and smart shoes lying in the coffin with his hands clasped together on his chest at his own funeral. I enjoyed my sister's company, but back then, I didn't understand the reason for her misanthropy, particularly of the youth. I asked her why she couldn't take me to the other side, where everyone else was going. Her excuse was the water was cleaner here. True, no one did their laundry and washed carpets, bathed their dogs and horses, or drowned their unwanted puppies at this secluded end. Few people admitted developing a rash from the contaminated water. When our Varvara started to go bald, Mama forbade her to frequent this recreation spot. She kept in line with this order, but as soon as the hair loss ceased, Varvara went back to her old habits.

Only when I started school, did I sympathise with Jelena's solitude. Everyone said we girls looked alike, whereas Felix with his slightly more European looks took after our Slavic mama. Looks are such an important part of every girl's personal perception of themselves, whether they admit that or not. My sisters' beauty didn't conform to the beauty standards of the time and place. Every girl finds her own way of dealing with their supposed lack of visual advantages, but Jelena went along with what others told her she was.

Before the school broke up for the winter holiday, students and pre-school age children dressed in hand-made costumes gathered to celebrate the festivities. Little ones would learn a few verses of some winter-themed poem in exchange for a bag of sweets from a man dressed as *Grandpa Frost*, for which their parents paid in advance. This red-nosed *Grandpa Frost* sometimes had a lady companion who was supposed to be his girlfriend - *The Snow Maiden*. *Grandpa Frost* was a golden-hearted, old, and forgetful man who loved to drink. He wore a long blue or red fur coat and had a staff he pretended to menacingly thump the floor with. His voice was menacingly deep and loud too, but we were meant to know he was only teasing us, really he was kind. *The Snow Maiden* was young and jolly, sometimes she scolded him and kept him in check. This dynamic was replaced with a single *Father Christmas* in a red and white costume in the new millennium.

This highly anticipated celebration was called a *Carnival*, and it was a great opportunity to get your pictures taken in front of the ceiling-high Christmas tree by a professional photographer. Our Mama stitched an adorable Polar Bear outfit for me. I began learning my verses two weeks before the *Carnival*. Jelena, Varvara, Felix, and I all went together but we never got our pictures done that day. Jelena's classmates ridiculed our intentions by voicing the usual racial slurs.

"Everyone look, the *Churkas'* family have come to get their photographs taken!"

It must have been my sister's ambition to eventually find herself among broad-minded people, which helped her bear the school every day. That, and Mama's heavy hand if she slipped. I think I can recall Mama confessing to me decades later, that sometimes she had no one else to take her own suppressed suffering out on. To defend her actions, she gave examples of families where parents drank and didn't look after their children, where mothers led a dissolute lifestyle, but those children never dared to rebuke their parents. On the contrary, they always returned to them with kindness. It didn't help that our chauvinist neighbour was Jelena's head-teacher. The Nineties was a dark period in the post-Soviet countries' history which would rather be forgotten by those people who didn't drink themselves to death or commit suicide. People like our neighbour did and said unkind things to people like my family because they knew they could.

When Jelena's classmates called her *Churka*, he sniggered. When the girls stuck chewing gum into her long, luscious hair, he chose to ignore it. When she graduated with distinction, he came to our home and dumped her certificate on the living room table without even congratulating her.

Mama told her to kick those girls in the cunt next time they attacked her - this would put them off forever.

The misery wasn't over for my eldest sibling. She was made to endure the most hurtful and gratuitous drops of power Papka still held. He couldn't use it on anyone else but the most vulnerable - his children. Jelena still didn't have a passport at the age of eighteen when she was supposed to have got one at sixteen. Not having the document prevented her from going to university or anywhere for that matter. When she attempted to get one the first time, Papka made a scene at the immigration office on the grounds of his personal contempt for Lithuania and its government's choice to leave the Soviet Union. He hadn't been a citizen of any country ever since and strongly opposed his children becoming one too. With obstinate and foolish pride, he refused to consent to Jelena obtaining her passport. Mother and daughter were in tears and found themselves imploring him to sign the documents. Eventually, he understood the consequences of his ludicrous action for his child and deigned to give parental consent. But he had to take pleasure in the cries and pleas of his family on two more occasions until this big and authoritative lady walked out of her room and asked him who the hell he thought he was.

Next, was scoring perfect marks in the exams. Achieving eight out of ten points in the crucial biology exam didn't suffice to secure a free spot in the medical university. Jelena was offered a place for a non-exorbitant fee, but any fee was exorbitant for this family. When my sister was five, she was prescribed glasses, but our parents couldn't afford them, and that was with both parents working. While her vision deteriorated, teachers allowed her to come close to the blackboard to write things down, because she couldn't see them. Only when she went to university could she buy her own prescription glasses. She used to watch TV with her index finger curled over her thumb – the OK sign – to be able to see. This always intrigued me, and I did the same, hoping to see what she was seeing. My sister still hoped that, in some miraculous way, her parents would be able to make some compromises to pay for her studies. Instead, she received a harsh punishment from Mama for failing to get in for free. On that unfortunate day when she shared the results, Mama hit her and pulled her hair. The remaining outstanding marks permitted Jelena to get into the University of Agriculture in the department of economics.

Chapter III

There were no jobs in the provinces, and everyone relied on their animal and field husbandry to sustain themselves. There were a few exceptions like my teacher-neighbours and people like Brigita's family. Nobody locked their door during the day, a neighbour would barge into your home to borrow sugar, a newspaper, make a telephone call if you could afford to have a landline, or simply to gossip. In summer, we would gather into small communities to help each other to harvest the hay, but that was before the spirit of the post-communist world started to diminish, and everyone began competing and picking their friends based on who owned better stuff. Hay season had always been a stressful time of the year if you didn't own your own harvesting transport. Mama chased tractor owners, entreating them to cut our hay at the start of the summer. At the outset nobody took her seriously and she was let down a few times. It was a husband's responsibility to make such arrangements, but Papka's poor Lithuanian language and social skills meant an uneven balance of responsibility and a complete absence of yang energy in their partnership. Severe sunburns and blistered hands were the aftermath of manual, old school hay raking. We'd head out in the morning taking some food and a lump of ice in the bottle to be drank when it melted.

Felix suffered a sun stroke when he was still a young boy, while his father worked away from home in mainly Russian-speaking regions of the country, where he felt more comfortable. Three women and a boy could have done with a pair of strong man's hands tending and baling hay, but no matter how hard these tasks were, they'd rather do it all themselves helped by other people, than by this man. Papka's view of the world differed from that of Mama's. Neither of them wanted to keep livestock and perform back- breaking jobs securing forage for it, but Mama knew that this was necessary to feed their children, whereas Papka cursed the cows for eating hay in winter. He arrived wearing a white, skimpy sports outfit when everyone else was sweating in the full swing of drudgery. He started insulting Mama for making him toil in the field, attempting to be witty with his nonsensical questions at the same time.

"Why do you need this much hay? Are you going to eat it all yourself?" No one thought he was remotely funny. "Shitty hay, shitty cows, shitty woman. I am a teacher! My back hurts!"

Laura's father - briefly turned sober and following the clean path for a while - was helping us that day when this happened. He said to my father "I can strengthen your ailing back with my pitchfork if that's what you're asking for". This silenced him, but he took it out on Mama later, as all men of his ilk do.

If the rain graced us from above, we'd huddle by the sheaves to wait for it to end. There were poor hay harvests when it all turned black because of so much rain. It wouldn't last the winter and Mama needed to ask people if they knew someone who was selling hay around the months of February and March. Animals in the fields needed to be tended to regardless of the weather. On one of the many stormy evenings, Mama went to milk the cows and didn't come back for ages. I'd like to say it was me who put a tiny raincoat on, and with torch in hand, stepped out to look for her, but I was too little to even remember this. It was my courageous brother, Felix, who felt too anxious just to sit at home wondering if Mama had got struck by lightning. He went to meet her halfway, while Papka wasn't bothered. He cursed the bad weather and preferred the sun and would much rather sunbathe in summer by the river than develop skin corns and calluses from the hard friction of the pitchfork handle in his hands. Laura's father kept a horse and would never refuse to help us transport the hay, straw, potatoes, or dung, when Mama asked him to. The only inconvenience was that the payment for the service would not be settled at the agreed price. Once the man was off the rails debauching, he'd send in Laura or his stepson Tadas to ask Mama for more money for a bottle, always late at night. When Mama refused this request, the father would come himself. Eventually Mama learned the lesson of never letting him in and never opening the door again. It's astonishing what addiction can do to a man. He'd ceaselessly ring the doorbell and if Mama's patience ran out and she yielded to the plea, her own honest response that she had no money to give him would simply fall on deaf ears.

A few times she emptied her purse of its last coins just to get rid of him. Many years after this, when I was already a teenager, Laura's half-brother escorted me to our pasture with his horse to collect the last of the hay, while the weather still permitted it. Papka was instructed to get there first to make the preparations. If it had been anyone other than that poor boy, when we stumbled on my father naked, soaking up the sun at the end of the field, I'd have prayed for the ground to swallow me up. But the knowledge that Tadas's stepfather was tons worse than my Papka, alleviated my embarrassment. He would heartlessly subject him to flogging, make him stand in the corner with his arms and legs spread in his briefs all night, and let him go to school starving.

The Luktuk family had as many children as my parents did, but they lived in a very large, commodious house on a hill with many rooms. I loved going there as I longed for us to own a house like that. It seemed to me that if every night, before drifting to the land of dreams, I vividly imagined the interior of our house to the last detail, it would become a reality. I dreamed of having my own room where I could stick posters of Leonardo Di Caprio and Kate Winslet on the walls. Before I discovered my other talents, drawing the layouts of the rooms and house plans were among my favourite things. 'Why don't they place the carpets on the floor?' I remember thinking to myself when we visited the Luktuk place 'Why is everything all over the place, why is it always a mess here? If I had my way, I'd tidy it all up and make it look nice,' I thought. Both Mr. and Mrs. Luktuk were given good dowries and hailed from the same village. Luktuk was an odious man even before he came back from Afghanistan in the eighties, irreversibly damaged. He refused to give his firstborn his last name and showed a lot of negative qualities, for which he earnt his in-law's disapproval of the marriage. During her speech at her daughter's wedding, the mother of Mrs. Luktuk infamously said, that God was a witness how much they didn't want him in their family. The man was greedy and just like everyone who had access to communal, state-owned resources through some cushy position during the communist reign, Mr. Luktuk built his family this house on a generous piece of land, managing the expenses via bureaucratic means. The era of wild capitalism ensued shortly afterwards, which made most people turn to alcohol. Mr. Luktuk, an electrician by trade, didn't escape this. The Luktuks kept a mare which proved to be a feeder of the family.

    Since we were poor, and the Luktuks were poor, we exchanged favours to help support each other's families. The Leaches also exchanged favours, but it was a little more difficult with them because of their many astute qualities that quickly set them apart from the rest of the community. The Luktuks were there for us when Mama couldn't get any tractor to collect our hay. Their mare hauled a cart laden with autumn harvest goods, potatoes, mangold, and cabbage from our fields, and carried back manure to fertilise the soil that our food grew on. We never had any money, but we were never hungry. Earning something of monetary value was a rare opportunity in the village, but you could make a little money if people knew they could hire you for a hay or harvest season, or any other task that they couldn't do themselves. Laura and Tadas's parents were usually employed for such tasks. There were apple orchards that still belonged to the state-owned structures and were free for people to pick the apples there. My siblings' textbooks and winter boots were bought with the money from those apples sales. The apple picking season was August to September, which was a great time to cover the school expenses just in time. The year Jelena finished school, Mama bought her a white blouse, a denim skirt, and a wristwatch because she owned very few fashion items. Mama was great at budgeting, even managing to scrape a small sum of money to give to Jelena before she went to university. She hoped Jelena would buy herself some nice garments, now that she was a student and lived in a big city, but instead, this selfless girl came back with a roll of wallpaper for our hall. She always tried to improve our abode, as she put it, to assuage the embarrassment of our poverty should unexpected guests decide to come by. I eagerly waited for those guests to arrive any time. I asked her who they would be. Jelena convinced my supple mind that those guests would come from the city and that they lived in better homes with better furniture, and that we must try our best to keep our home tidy. In those early days of my existence, all I heard was her telling me not to break or damage stuff at home, asking me to be more careful with something because we still owed money to someone for that item. I think sometimes it was true, taking things on credit was very common. The villagers sold and bought things from one another on a collect now, pay later basis. I can't help thinking that in my case, it was just a great way to subdue my exuberant conduct at home.

I was five years old when my favourite sister left home. No one explained anything to me until the day she had to leave. I burst into tears and just like our cat, Vasily, I hid under Mama's bed and didn't stop howling "Jelena!" for hours. She left. I quickly got over it. For the next two years until I started school, playing games with Felix brought out rather boyish qualities in me. I could not expect him to play home-making games with me, naturally, I had to fight him on the battlefield with soldiers, tanks, and paper ships that he taught me to fold. You fold it the same way as you would a hat. It's the only thing I can fold from paper today.

People ask me, "Oh, you do origami?"

And I'd say "No, just that one thing."

Whenever my forces faced his, I would lose each time. I waited for Felix to come home from school, to have lunch and feed the cows in the shed. He would then spend a couple of hours destroying my invading army before proceeding to his homework. We created this half cat, half human character called Boris, who carried a loaf of bread under his arm and walked with a cane in his other hand. Eventually it evolved into two cats called Boris, one was Felix's, another one mine. Since then, we competed to see whose Boris was tougher, richer and more successful, by putting them into each other's stories where one was proved to be better than the other one. Needless to say, Felix would win that competition too.

Although I must admit, thanks to this, my wit and imagination were spurred to come up with funny story lines and jokes from an early age.

No one else could fathom our banter and the warped sense of humour that only the two of us shared. Felix taught me how to play chess and checkmated me every time we played, except one time when I won. Two times I flung the chess board down in a childish rage about losing to him again. The first time he laughed, and I felt good about myself for making my big brother laugh. I only flung the board down the second time to receive the same reaction. I wasn't angry at all, but to my dismay, he got annoyed with me and said he wouldn't play if I did such things. I didn't do it again. There was a long cabinet, stretching across most of the living room wall; we kept our books, china, glassware and linen in it. If you went around people's homes, you would find the same cabinet in their living rooms, stacked with the same type of items, except books. You would definitely not find any literature in poor Almantas's living room cabinet. Once a good son, he yielded to his overbearing mother's suffocating love and never married a woman.

He married drink instead, lived with his mother and was called by a diminutive name, Almutis by everyone in the village. No woman was ever good enough to be with her son, his mother said, thus ensuring her life's biggest fear of losing him would never come true and he would never have his chance to be a fulfilled man. Over the years she developed another fear, that of her son's drunken bellow and fists in her face. Deprived of happiness, he engaged in an inebriated and bitter struggle with the world. In a drunken stupor, he broke into the neighbours' flat, ate their lunch, and wet their couch in his sleep. He told everyone that the wife of this neighbour shouted so loudly that he could hear her through the wall between them, and two of those long living room cabinets. Almutis encapsulated everything that mothers didn't wish to happen to themselves or to their sons. They harmlessly teased their silly boys with this diminutive name like a bogeyman if those young men showed no interest in the opposite sex when they ought to have. While Felix was still a little boy, he made a promise never to marry and to live with his Mama and buy her a Cadillac like Elvis Presley. "You will look out of the window, Mama and see the car I bought you" he used to say to her.

Varvara and Felix were allocated a shelf each in the cabinet to store their trifles, which gave them a sense of identity. I also wanted to have a shelf when I was older and knew that once Varvara went to College, I'd inherit her shelf, and maybe even some of that nonsensical but very valuable junk of hers.

Maybe, maybe not. I didn't dismiss this idea, she was a girl and one day I'd be interested in that stuff too, but I wasn't in a rush to grow into a girly girl yet and found my brother's possessions piqued my interest more. Versatile and talented, Felix earned the reputation of a painter at school and was entrusted to paint Jesus on the cross and play Gomez in the school's Addams Family production in his later years. He also became popular with girls. Everyone said to me that my brother was really handsome. In particular, my future classmate, Milana's mother, passed on her shameless, lustful views of my fine brother to her daughter, who later used this to make her point that it was okay if I wasn't good-looking, my brother was. Milana was simple-minded because her mother drank and smoked while pregnant with her. Our Mama was happy that Felix resembled her and not his father. The fallacy that sons take after their mother and daughters after their father was rife in our community.

"We girls are not attractive at all, we look like our father. Thankfully the boy turned out a tiny bit better looking." Jelena spouted to me once, in a high-pitched and exasperating tone of tone that she used to compel me to abase myself. It was only in my adolescence that my sister began to loathe the disparity in our characters but she never succeeded in bringing me down. Her sentiments were never believable to me, and therefore I never felt hurt by them however hard she tried.

The obvious proof that a boy was popular with girls was when he could get hold of something that belonged to a girl. In the same way, throwing her into the river also meant that a boy liked that girl. The older Leach daughter got thrown in a lot. If you have also ever wondered what the mystery is behind the charm plain women hold over men, I think it's because these women have better personalities. The oldest Leach was the nicest and least selfish of all her sisters. If a girl was still dressed and saw a guy approaching her, she knew what was coming, but she could not fight him as he was physically superior. However, she must resist, beg him not to try running, he might get some reinforcement from his friends to hurl her over the promenade before she got swung into the water. She acted like she didn't want to, but it was just a charade really, because for that one moment, she was the centre of everyone's attention and it was clear as day that guys found her attractive. The logic behind this was simple, those young lads didn't touch unappealing girls. The more times you were cast into that river against your will, the more popular you were.

A girl forfeiting a personal item meant that the girl didn't mind that boy having something of hers, she felt flattered that he wanted it, and he, that she gave it to him. Of course, she acted like she didn't, and begged him not to take her ring or her hair band, or her pen or a bracelet. She would feign a struggle against him. This exchange of sympathy would only happen between popular girls and boys. Felix managed to obtain a few cheap necklaces and rings with fake stones that he kept in a crude wooden box he had made. Some meagre amounts of change were also kept in that box, secured with a heavy lock as big as the box itself. He would deliberately open it in front of me to further engage my curiosity by exaggerating the value of his treasure. My imagination had no limits, and so I found a screwdriver to unscrew the hinges with and opened the box. I waited for him to return from school and enormously pleased with the fruits of my operation, I showed my brother and Mama how clever I was.

Bemused, I received a very painful but deserved belt punishment. Good parents have a duty to display and cultivate the correct moral values in their offspring. I didn't want the stuff in the box, I just wanted my brother to see that I could bypass that huge lock to open his treasure.

This minor misunderstanding didn't put a dampener on our relationship, and I continued admiring many of my big brother's abilities. In my childish eyes, he was the man of the house. I followed him anywhere I could. Every year Felix would bring a real Christmas tree for us. It was not permitted by law to cut down the trees in the woods, hence everyone was careful when and how they did it so as not to get caught, even though every household got their trees from the same place. The last thing you needed was to look like an oaf for getting a fine for something so trivial and silly as bringing home a Christmas tree for your family. Even our Woods Ranger knew what was going on, but you had better not get caught red-handed anyway. To me it was a lot of fun tagging along with my brother and chatting away while he chose the right tree and got down to the job. Felix told me to wriggle my toes when my feet felt cold.

I'd jump around a lot and let him answer my childish questions. I'd ask him when we were going to our grandfather's in Kaliningrad. Just like Jelena, he'd feed me harmless promises to make me do something. Usually, to behave well or fulfill my little obligations. Our grandfather was a widower and World War Two veteran. Mama often extolled his deeds of valour and immeasurable fortitude during the war to her friends. I'd often hear that he starved for nine-hundred days in the Leningrad siege, but such words held no meaning to me yet. Talk of war was for old people.

My granddad was a formidable character, and I didn't want to be left alone with him. He asked me questions in Russian and I always lost my tongue around my Russian relatives. Mama and Papka only spoke in Russian at home, but we always responded back in Lithuanian. It's this bizarre mixture of confusion and shyness that puts off most children from engaging in their parents' language, when it's different to the one everyone else is speaking around them.

Anything different and unfamiliar intimidates and puzzles children and even some adults, which explains why individuals get mocked if they stand out from the community.

I loved my cousins very much and wanted to be close to them. When I had an opportunity of a lifetime, literally, to play with them, my fear of speaking Russian took over and I scared the hell out of them by testing my lung capacity. In a terrified voice, I began spluttering to Felix in Lithuanian some unintelligible drivel that killed the playful vibe of the game they were engaged in, and he had to calm me down.

How I wished my relatives lived in Lithuania and came to visit us. I wanted to be like everyone else. I wanted my family to be like everyone else's. I wanted my friends and neighbours to know I also had cousins, an aunt, and an uncle. And I also wanted other children to stop telling me I looked different to them and to stop the new kids who didn't yet know me staring at me. Everyone else had grandmothers they used to stay with for the summer. I wanted to be taken to my Russian half-grandmother, my Mama's aunt, Baba Toma we called her, and left at hers for the entire summer, so I could come back to my village and brag about it. I could also make up some events that had happened to me and nobody could accuse me of lying, because there was no way they could have checked it. Our real grandmother, Varvara, in whose honour my sister had been named, had passed away when Jelena was just three years old. Baba Toma, short for Tamara, filled that important void in our lives. Being able to show others that I had an extended family seemed to me to provide some sort of status, and there is no wonder that I kept hassling my older siblings about when we would go to see them next; those trips to Kaliningrad were very scarce and very short.

One of my brother's idiosyncrasies was to never let me or anyone else decorate the Christmas tree. I so wanted to, but not even Mama could persuade him. She could only mollify my sobs. She said Felix was just like her own father: oddly possessive over Christmas tree decorations. Each time it happened, she gave a warm smile and took pleasure in the apparent similarities between her son and her father. She'd say "Just let him do it. He's just like granddad Alexey."

Luckily for everyone in the family, my good-looking brother resembled his own father very little in character too. He never shied away from physical work and since being a little boy, wished to improve the quality of life for his sisters and mother. One utterly broke Christmas, he emptied his savings fund and bought everyone small presents. I was too little to remember, and probably didn't get any, but Mama so often felt emotional when retelling this story in years to come. She was given a dog comb, which she kept. Quite frankly, I doubt anyone would ever be able to tell the difference between human hair and a dog fur comb. Although, where I live now, there are almost as many pampered dogs as humans, so probably those people would be able to tell the difference, but not back then, in my village, where lice-ridden mongrels were tethered to their kennels to serve an important function. Even so, Mama was ahead of her time to distinguish the combs. Since we were old enough to begin to observe the social standards that define the values of different groups of people, but not old enough to attach too much importance to it, our mother emphasised her highly superior and cultured background in stark contrast to the man she had married, and almost everyone who lived around us.

My granddad, Alexey, came from a wealthy horse breeders' family, who in the tradition of the times, owned land in a small village in the European part of Russia. His oldest brother who had studied in Paris, went to document the First World War on his camera, wrote letters to his family about how much he missed Mother Russia and hung out with prominent poets like Sergei Esenin. The twentieth century history of the Russian people had been testing and the fortune of the families as such was seized by the Bolsheviks.

"My parents loved me, but they had nothing to give me", he used to say, "Mother would pack one hot potato each for my older sister and me to take to school, but we were so hungry that we couldn't wait until our lunch time, so we'd stop on the way and eat them."

Being the youngest and born in the turbulent times of the country, my granddad was twenty-one and fresh from the Kronshtadt Navy School, when he was sent to Leningrad, days before the eight hundred- and eighty-two-day siege imposed by the Nazis and their Finnish allies ensued. The eerie sound of the metronome pendulum swing was already being transmitted on the city speakers when his regiment got there. This clicking sound became the heartbeat of the city and alerted the residents to a bombardment or a stand-off. Four of his older brothers had already died in the first days of the war in forty-one, and having come so close to death, when the heavy weight of a healthy-faced German soldier in a good uniform was felt on the top of his sinewy body, pressing down his Nazi fingers on my granddad's throat, the unwavering human desire to survive prevailed. My grandfather bit through the vein of the enemy's throat after he had unsuccessfully attempted to use the only weapon he had on him - a knife. After the dismal nine hundred days of starvation, my hero grandfather was deployed in the battle of Koenigsberg in the last months of the war.

"I pinched my ear to feel my own warm blood, because I couldn't believe that the fire had finally ceased and I could hear the waves of the Baltic Sea breaking ashore of the Curonian Spit." I heard my mother repeating_ these words so many times as well as "There were no atheists in the War." Hearing stories of my granddad Alexey's life, I couldn't imagine him being a young man, it was somehow a weird idea, but these words have left an indelible imprint on my memory. When the War ended, he paved his own path in life, thanks to his deep common sense, tenacity, and the life-long recognition by the Soviet State for his efforts in defending the homeland. He often said that if it wasn't for the War, he could have achieved success in some academic subject, and that everything would have been okay if there had been no war.

My grandma was a teenage girl during the War and together with her five-year old sister, Tamara, and mother, she was force-marched by the Nazis from Smolensk to Ukraine. They embarked in November and halted in April, never reaching their destination. Tamara was too young to understand what was happening and kept asking her mother to carry her, but the mother couldn't carry her, she was weak and could barely drag her own feet. Those who didn't keep up with the pace got shot where they stood. My grandmother was twelve and suffered the freezing, dire winter wading through the thick snow like an adult woman. She was conscious of the horror of the situation they were in. At her deathbed, my grandmother asked for forgiveness from her sister for yelling at her, because the little one kept asking their mother to be taken in her arms when the Germans forced them to march.

My granddad always held an important post in the community they lived in. People would come for his advice and tell their problems to him. Often, he'd lose his temper with people, including with his family. He was an impetuous man, but not an angry man. Grandma Varvara would console her daughter when she'd get into the firing-line for something very trivial.

"Don't be upset with your father. He's seen things that we haven't." He always made up for his fits of anger later by giving his women presents or money to buy themselves something nice. It was unwonted to talk about your feelings. My grandparents were tough but fair parents to their children. They taught them high discipline and respect for their elders, etiquette, the value of hard work, and one thing that my Mama later said she wished they hadn't - selflessness. She said the real reason why she ended up where she was in life, with my father, was because her parents didn't teach her how not to let others walk over her. I think the real reason she ended up with my father was because she fell in love with him, and when she fell out of love, it was too late.

Chapter IV

We kept and cared for our farm animals. We got attached to them, we named them and talked to them. We worried about them and nursed them when they were sick.

Mama murmured a quick prayer and made a sign of the cross before she left them for a night; I emulated her later. We hoped that the cows, Maya and Violet, would withstand the storms and torrid heat in the pastures in summer, and that their offspring wouldn't get torn apart by wolves or worse, cattle thieves, who very often would be someone we knew and said hello to. When you learnt that those people had stolen the calf that you had nurtured, given a name to, and looked forward to selling for a generous rate to a slaughterhouse, so you could afford clothes and boots for your children, you felt violated and helpless, because they had betrayed you and made you a part of their grubby plan. We got attached to our animals, we loved them, we ate them.

I knew that the meat I ate was of our stock: pigs, poultry, rabbits. I remember seeing those animals in a cowshed and interacting with them, like the chicks and geese that I tended when they were small. Then I would come back the next day and they wouldn't be there anymore. I remember how perplexed I was when one of our chickens got pressed to death by Violet. I have seen what a flat chicken looks like. Felix guffawed at my calling it a flat chicken. We shoveled it out with the rest of Violet's poop, there was nothing that could have been done for her, she was dead flat. One day I went to 'bring the rabbit home' with Felix. Blissfully ignorant, I regaled him with my childish enthusiasm, when he took one of our rabbits' head-down and started hitting it with the side of his palm, while holding the rabbit by its feet. Aghast at this horrid sight, I began screaming at him, asking him to stop hurting the rabbit and then ran off to hide away from this.

The second time, I felt the same hurtful emotions was when Laura's father was asked to slaughter our pig. Usually, a few days before the weekend Mama wanted to have the pig slaughtered, she would send one of us to pass the message on and confirm the hour with him. We had to remind him the night before in case he got carried away with his drinking spree. Mama would tell him off in advance.

"Please, don't let me down and get drunk, okay?"

He'd assure her "My sweet little girl, did I ever let you down?"

I think Laura's dad fancied my Mama, for once, when Papka had beaten her and I couldn't get her off the ground, I went to get him. I cried and begged Mama to get on her feet, but it wasn't her physical injuries that stopped her, it was her broken heart being broken again. Laura's dad scooped her off the floor and helped me take her to bed. He said if she was his wife she would never have to work. When I told Mama this, she said if she was his wife, she'd be hiding from him in a sheaf of hay at night, like his poor, petite wife did.

The killing would happen on a weekend when there was no school and everyone could help. The man would come with his wife, a short and lively woman of much potential and resourcefulness, stunted by alcohol addiction. Mama said that Laura's mother had loving parents who dressed her in nice dresses but then she married Laura's dad. This and similar stories would always be finished with 'Women cannot handle alcohol the same way men do. That is why women shouldn't drink. At first they think it's a conscious choice, then you find them lying in their own urine in a ditch. The deterioration is quicker for women. There is no happiness in the family where a mother is an alcoholic.'

There were few men in the village who knew how to execute a pig slaughter, but even fewer knew how to aim accurately at the hapless animal's heart. Laura's father wasn't that man. That day my task was to continue bringing warm water to the scene of the action. On one of the trips back, I heard the most piercing and excruciating scream of the dying pig. It was held down by several people on the black make-shift table, with the executioner unsuccessfully trying to end its suffering. The pig squealed and squealed; it was unbearable. I joined it in its cry.

Someone in the group, some of the neighbours who were there to help, found my cries cute and laughed at me. After the animal had released its last breath, its skin was roasted by the flamethrower and washed with warm water. The body was chopped into parts and taken home to preserve it. Laura's mum would remain on the site to cleanse the pig's intestines to make them into sausages later. The slaughter was finished by afternoon. Mama would give them their share of the meat, as well as pay them a little in money and beer. If she had no money that day, this would be expected to be remitted on one of those late night errands by Laura and Tadas.

In the days that followed, Mama busied herself with processing the mince, stuffing the freezer with the portions of meat, cooking and preserving the jars, and soaking the loins in endless baths of salt for two weeks, before they could be finished in a smokehouse. We didn't have a smokehouse, hence arrangements needed to be made with a neighbour who owned one. We would be sorted for months until new piglets were bought and fattened, only to follow the fate of their predecessors.

The year I was born, our entire meat supply was stolen from the smokehouse just before Christmas. With bitter tears Mama cried out "You people are a nation of thieves!" to which someone responded with:

"Like you don't have thieves in Russia?"

"Russians didn't come last night to take my children's food away from them, did they?" Whoever it was, they knew us, and we said hello to them, and without a doubt we continued talking to them and greeting them. As my granddad said to my Mama, when she told him on the phone that our beautiful, ginger calf Ugnele had been lured away from our pasture at night and slaughtered in the woods nearby:

"There are thieves in this world and their function is to steal." So, there were always people who lived by the sweat of their brow and there were always thieves. My granddad had been robbed of a large amount of cash once.

He had come home earlier than usual and out of the corner of his eye he saw this guy he knew hiding behind another door.

Granddad gave a vague impression that he was missing something in his pockets, so he left his flat immediately until much later the same day, thus allowing the thief to extricate himself from the crime scene. The money was gone. My grandfather didn't go to the authorities. He didn't confront the perpetrator. He continued talking to that man and saying hello to him. A thief is a thief, regardless of race or nationality.

Ugnis in Lithuanian means fire or flame. Ugnele is a diminutive word to say, "a little flame, a little fire". What I loved about calves most was their minuscule, growing horns on top of their long, narrow heads. Cow offspring must find the development of their horns very itchy because they always try to rub that part of their heads onto something. They also release low, chesty proto-moo sounds. The link between little calves and baby bears has always been vivid in my head. Cubs and calves would be my preference to a dog or cat, but they never stay small. I cannot recall whether Ugnele was Maya's or Violet's daughter. |Neither of them was ginger. The birth of a calf was anticipated with great excitement and trepidation. Shortly before its arrival, Mama, Felix, or Papka would have to get up a few times at night and with a torch in their hands head down to the cowshed to check if the mother cow had delivered her baby.

When this happened, they would come back with a loaf of dark-rye bread, loads of salt and a tub of warm water. I would have to go to see this bundle of joy first thing in the morning. The poor things struggled to stand on their feeble, slender legs at first, but they would grow fast in no time. Clumsy, adorable, little funny things they were.

However scant our finances were, Mama always saved a loaf of bread for the cow close to its due time. We children knew it and didn't touch it, but Papka would trawl through Mama's underwear drawers to find it and stuff his bottomless abyss. In tears and fury, my mother kept asking him what was wrong with him and went to the shop to ask for bread on credit. It wasn't just the bread for the cows she hid from him, she saved it for us too; if she hadn't, there would be none left.

Ugnele's demise had taken place this one typically warm Lithuanian summer when Mama and Felix were renovating the flat. Summer was the ultimate home improvement season for many people. Felix had learned how to do most of those kind of jobs by the age of sixteen, mostly by observing Mr. Leach and other grown-up men in the neighborhood. Mr. and Mrs. Leach teased him and called him their son-in-law. Our ginger lady was flourishing and turning into a fine, healthy heifer. Mama had already drafted a budget of the costs that her sale would cover and was in a rare good mood. I think Mama was only ever in a good mood when there were house improvements involved.

Her eyes would glimmer with passion when she talked about installing a fireplace, changing doors and windows, redecorating the rooms and a bathroom, and reconstructing her preposterously small kitchen, where two people were a crowd. She always dreamed of ripping down the wall between our kitchen and the storage room to expand the kitchen. This was what other neighbours in our house had done and Mama went to look at it and agreed that it did make a difference. Everyone felt that they must invest in their homes and whenever they saved up enough money, something old would be changed into something new. Then they would invite the neighbours to evaluate these changes and talk excessively about the costs. Contacts for the master-builders would be exchanged. And so, one early summer morning, Mama went to the pastures to milk the cows and found that Ugnele wasn't there. It must have been a surreal moment for Mama because she refused to accept that the calf must have been murdered by now. Those living nearby were organised into search groups, the police were involved and very soon, what remained of Ugnele was discovered in the surrounding forest. Our police chief obliquely pointed out the most likely perpetrator, but very unfortunately, nothing could be proved. The same people had stolen and eaten our chickens as recently as a few years before this incident. The police chief implied that the man who did it was preparing to get wed that summer, and had therefore picked our calf to be served to his guests on his wedding table. For many years to come, Mama would bitterly repeat the police chief's words;

they made more sense after everyone discovered the main instigator of a shameful and ludicrous blackmailing affair of our school head teacher. It was indeed the same man. This man was Varvara's classmate and always embarrassed her at the village discos when he asked her out for a dance. He was a short, skinny, epileptic boy who often confused reality with his imaginary world where he was a secret police agent one day, the next one he was a member of a very influential mafia ring, and to convince everyone, he dangled the same gun he had somehow got hold of. The gun was probably not real either.

Those blissful pre-school days couldn't have passed any more languidly for an agile child like me. I enjoyed my own company playing, locked up in the flat while my siblings were at school and Mama tended to the livestock. I had many toys, but the most coveted ones were a Barbie doll and a piano pencil case that took over the households with children by storm, in the nineties. Greta Leach had one, of course. Mama gave in to my pleas and bought me a green piano pencil case out of love and a wish to see me happy, even though I could name at least three better things she could have spent that money on. Because I experienced happiness more intensely than normal children, I broke things easily with my strong Slavic-Mongolian grip. She bought me another pencil case; I didn't let it out of my hands all day and by the evening of the same day it was broken. Barbie dolls didn't last in my ownership too long either. In my defence, if you asked someone what their first association was with China back then, they would have to say, 'things break easily'. It was true. This was the time when provincial stores started filling up with things manufactured in China that became more and more accessible to common people, but you still needed to have the wherewithal to buy them. They were colourful, plastic, often cartoon and pop-culture themed, the most desirable out of all junk that had "Made in China" labelled on them.

Two instances stand out in my memory from those solitary mornings playing with my toys. I couldn't develop any feelings for our little black dog, Aris, and I wasn't devastated when he later passed away from some sort of illness. He made me cry and hide in the cupboard armed with a poker after I saw him greedily chewing on my Barbie. I heard the key turn in the door lock and ran straight to my Mama, longing to be pitied. Another time, playing alone had gone on for a long time and it was approaching lunch for I had started to feel hungry when the same key in the door turned and Mama stumbled in, supported by the kind neighbour. Mother's headscarf was drenched in blood. My shriek was stalled by terror, but the neighbour's calm demeanour soothed the situation for both of us. She told me that Maya had hit Mama in the face, and she had fallen between the two cows and a young bull and lain there unconscious for some time before recovering herself and scrambling out for help. Everyone else had already milked and fed their cows and pigs by this time, but by a rare stroke of luck, that lady was walking by when she found and helped my Mama.

Mama always said that God didn't let the cattle trample her and saved her from dying that day, because she still had me to bring up. She also said that a cow is like a person. It has a character of its own that needs to be reckoned with. Indeed, women in the community were conscious of May's impulsive character when asked to milk her if Mama was ill or away.

Chapter V

The only thing I'm grateful to my father for is my ability to read from the early age of five. Paradoxically, he never managed to advance his Lithuanian beyond beginner's level, but it sufficed to teach me how to connect the syllables into words. First came the headlines of the newspaper articles. *The Confrontation* was my practice piece on many occasions until Mama saw that I required a different type of literature. She paid for my monthly young adults' magazine of crosswords, spot the difference, connect the dots, labyrinth games, riddles, short stories, and articles to my liking and plenty of beautiful pictures. There weren't any easy books in our home library that I could read, so I went to the village library and expressed my intention of getting my reader's card there. The librarian scoffed at me, but I demonstrated how adept I was at reading the book covers, which was enough to assure her that I could be trusted to take books home. I was only asked not to brag about it to other six-year-olds. Next, I began my lessons with one of the primary school teachers living downstairs. I would go to her flat for an hour of reading, writing and maths. Everyone told me she would be my year one teacher from September. She was once married to our school head teacher, although the marriage was ephemeral, for he sneaked out with half of everything they owned together, including china and cutlery, while she was at work. The woman maintained a dignified composure and continued working in the same school despite all the rumours that she was barren, which was why her husband had left her. People nicknamed her former husband, Arab, because of his thick black moustache. Since then he became friendly with Jelena's biology teacher. They sang together in the church choir and performed in the same community group. My excitement about starting school that year was through the roof. Mama put on a birthday party for me and invited Mrs. Leach with Greta and my future teacher. She brought me a battery-operated toy microphone. Ten more years passed before I had another birthday party like that again. That day Greta was cordial to me and allowed me to take centre stage. We played in front of the three ladies and were conscious of being watched while they used the spectacle as a starting point for their conversation. Life felt truly good to me.

Diligently, I attended all my school preparation lessons with my teacher and together with Mama, I hoped to be ahead of everyone else in my class. This wasn't meant to happen until the following September.

The school said I couldn't be accepted because I was only six and the two classes for year one were full already, which meant that I would have a different teacher too. Was I sad? I cannot remember. My lessons ceased but I continued going to the library and returning books every week.

Sometimes Mama asked me to bring her some Russian books. The kind librarian made her recommendations.

Papka's return home on the payday weekend was always an event which caused ambivalent feelings to the family. If we knew he was coming, we would wait for the bus arrival hour and go to meet him at the bus stop. He wouldn't get out of that bus if he had missed it and had to sleep at the train station in Vilnius until the next service again. My siblings and I looked forward to the presents in his big sports bag more than anything else, really. Varvara would put in her request in advance for whatever she wanted him to buy her; always some fashion item that she saw the Leach or other girls at school wear. He bought her a sequined hair bow once, and a green velvet dress that she later cut into pieces for a fashion show at school. Mama was livid.

Varvara's purchases were one of the things our parents argued about. Mama saw it as an utter waste of money, Papka had no discernment. All I cared about was my monthly *Donald Duck* comic magazines that Papka picked up at the newsagent's kiosk before coming home. Mickey never did it for me, Donald Duck with his significant other, his three nephews, a stingy uncle, Scrooge McDuck, and Cousin Phillip, were my favourite characters. The illustration filters in those magazines took me to my happy place. I imagined it to be always sunny, with palm trees, tall city buildings, wide streets filled with cars. Lots of colour. I longed to be in a place like that and didn't ask for anything else. Felix and Varvara, on the other hand, started their little chewing gum sales venture at school. Papka would buy a few boxes of those things, in fancy, shiny plastic wrappers. Chewing gum was a novelty in the provinces in those years. What prompted my family members to start their business, was actually a very petty act from a shop owner in our village. He gladly gave away empty boxes to the Leach girls to play with. Empty boxes of chewing gum. The girls were showing off and piqued childish jealousy in Varvara and Felix. Mama told them to go to the same man and ask for the boxes.

When they did, he refused them. It was Mama's suggestion that they should ask their father to bring them some bubble gum from the city. Chewing gum turned out to be a valuable currency to pay the Luktuk children for their mare's services.

Father's visit would usually start off well. We'd surround him to receive the gifts and while still elated, usually I would be handed the stash of money to take to Mama in another room. Mama would pour out a big bowl of soup and ask me to tell father to come to get it. He would be left alone to eat in our poky kitchen, with Mama nagging him that the money was not enough to pay all the bills, to buy enough food to last until the next pay date, not to mention the footwear and clothes for us. I would hear her say that no one else has a rusty old bathtub like we do, and that we need to get a boiler, and the stove needs repairing, that it will end up collapsing and killing someone. She'd always use the Leaches to draw a distinction between us and them, and she'd talk about Mr. Leach's ability to earn enough money and fix things, so that Mrs. Leach did not have to worry about the things that my mother had to.

Mr. Leach never had an official job, both his wife and he came from very humble backgrounds. Both their mothers were alcoholic, and they had doubtful paternal origins. There had been every chance of them falling into the same pattern of life choices if it had not been for their endless resourcefulness and aspiration to elevate themselves from poverty. Mama said that one time they were all going to the welfare and benefits office in town, when someone asked Mr. Leach where he had learned all the building and repairing skills he had, and he answered, "Life has taught me."

Later I wondered whether Mama really expected our father to suddenly change and become more like her friend's husband one day? Did she really believe that if she continually compared her daughters to the Leaches, we would want to be more like them? To this her answer was "It is better be led by some real-life example."

Papka would want to sit down and read a newspaper, he loved collecting newspapers, but Mama insisted he put on his work overalls and go out to do some jobs. He hated getting his hands dirty and ignored her the first few times, until provoked, she started yelling at him. This would often escalate into loud arguments. He'd tell her that he was a teacher, and his job was to teach and not shovel shit. She'd retort that his teacher colleagues in our house earnt more than him and had higher qualifications, but still didn't shy away from getting down to the gritty jobs. When she'd be done exalting Mr. Leach, she'd use the chauvinist neighbour downstairs.

"He works forty hours at school, probably brings home about two thousand a month, he doesn't even need to dig the soil, but you never see him sitting and reading newspapers. He's a teacher but he's somehow managed to build his second garage and a garden shed from scratch. And you, what did you ever build? A few wonky shelves in a storage that fell off the next day." Facts.

"I'm so sick of your cows, your pigs and hay." This was evident through the beating marks on our pigs and the fear emanating from the assaulted animals at the sight of him.

"Your children would be dead of starvation if it wasn't for me. You don't complain when you stuff your bag with that food, do you?" Felix wanted to walk Papka to the bus stop, but Papka would politely refuse so he could steal down to the cellar and sneak in a few jars of marinated meat and vegetables.

"Papka," I asked him once "why do you bring those empty egg boxes with you?"

"Oh, that's to carry some organic eggs back with me." We only had a few skinny hens.

Mama said that if there was a famine, he would eat his own children. Very rightly so, mother expressed her astonishment that her father had survived on two hundred and fifty grams of bread in the Leningrad blockade and would give every bite out of his mouth to his offspring, but the man she married was not like her father. This man was born after the second World War in a hut in some obscure Kazakh village and was separated from his parents when he was just eight months old. Nobody knew exactly when he was born, his date of birth was brought forward to the new year, as a part of accepted practice. He was raised by his maternal grandmother and when she was too old to care for him, he went to a state boarding school. Perhaps the constant shortage of food and rationing, an empty stomach, and a struggle to defend your portion from other growing lads, was forever reflected in my father's concern to look after his own interests. He told us that he had watched TV for the first time at twelve and tasted cabbage for the first time when served in the army. He also said he used to pretend to be sick at school to get slightly more food.

"At least he is not fussy about what he eats," Mama consoled herself. Indeed, he wasn't.

There was not much on Papka's mind besides food, the desire to remain as young as possible, outlive all of us and move back to Kazakhstan for a second round of children with a younger wife. She would be gentle and meek, and they would read poetry and newspapers to each other.

"How many times did I tell you to move to the city with me? We would have been given a nice flat." Like every argument in the world, this one also never reached any resolution.

"If I was like your father, you, my children, would now be looking for food in bins or living in an orphanage." She'd say. I was terrified of having to live in an orphanage and she milked my childish trepidation because it didn't work with her older children. "If I died, only my little one would cry for me."

In the end, our father would have to do some jobs. He and Felix would go to the woods, to prepare some logs. "Son, have you got a chainsaw?" he'd ask.

"I do." Felix hankered to hang out with the masculine figure.

"What about an axe?"

"I took an axe too."

"Untether the dog then," this last instruction was overheard by Mama who interrupted.

"For the love of God, would you unleash the dog, you lazy old git! Do something!" Mama yelled.

Our father was far from a paradigm father figure, and we all toyed with the idea of what would happen if Mama took us and left him. There was always some other event that needed to occur before that one could take place: too many of us were of school age. Jelena had to graduate, there were a few more years until Varvara finished school and then two more years for Felix. Once they were partially off our mother's back, there was only one minor that Mama would be fully responsible for. She would move to Russia, but then I'd need to go to Lithuanian school.

"I'm only waiting for you to turn eighteen." That's what my father used to say to me, and then giggled, expecting me to laugh with him. "Then I wouldn't have to pay your support money."

A long time ago my mother and father slept in the same bed and locked the door to be alone in the flat. I don't recall those days. My birth marked the beginning of banal arguments about food and money, and stripped and reduced their marriage to survival mode.

Everyone in my family has at least one bright memory associated with the days of Papka working away from home. One of my brother's must be the time when he was taken to the capital, to Vilnius, for a few days.

Mama tried to dissuade him - he had nothing to wear. Boys of that age sprout so quickly. Their wardrobes need frequent updating. Felix remained adamant. So what that his trousers and jacket sleeves were too short on him, he was going to the city with his father. He asked Papka to take him to *McDonald's*. Despite his unfulfilled expectations, the journey left a big impression on my big brother. They wandered around the city and went to a bank for no reason. When staff asked if they could help, Papka said "We just came to have a look. Thanks." They did go to McDonald's, but the same thing happened there. Papka got intimidated by the attentive personnel, so he took Felix by the hand and walked out. In a children's playground, Papka told Felix to go down the slide with the five-year-olds.

"Go, son, have a go at it." Felix was twelve.

Then they went to the train station where with the tramps and other questionable characters, Papka felt the most comfortable. Felix told us that a woman came up to them and invited Papka to come with her to her room, where she had soap and shampoo. We kept retelling the same story out loud among ourselves over and over, without knowing what it was really about. When we did so, Papka told us to stop it.

There was also a weird encounter with a man and his son. It was as if Papka had met his twin. They bought and read newspapers and started passing judgment on the articles they read, which brought them together and thus they spent the waiting time discussing politics.

By the time father had to go back, something unpleasant and sad would have happened, which marred the experience every single time.

I was woken up by mother's sobs at night.

Since Jelena had moved out, the four of us shared the room. I slept with Mama and Felix and Varvara had a bunk bed. Father always slept in the living room on the floor, along the piano by the kafel wall oozing heat. He'd sleep with his entire face buried under the covers, which wouldn't muffle his horrendous snores. Everyone else seemed impervious to the snivels coming out of the storage unit. I got up and knocked on the door. I couldn't push it in because she held it with her back against it. It didn't take me long to start crying with her. There was something very wrong with my mother.

With my older siblings ostensibly deep in sleep. I don't know how long I sat by that door begging her to open it. Papka appeared in his white washed-out boxer shorts and told me to go back to bed but I refused. Without much trying he went back to his lodging as if he had just been going through the motions.

Why was everyone so ignorant of our mother's unhappiness? She opened the door. A deep, red mark was encircling her neck. Don't ask me how I knew the meaning of this skin imprint on her neck. A child's mind is like a sponge that absorbs everything it hears around them, every word uttered by the adults, every story about people dying of their own hands leaves a vivid image in the memory of that child. We embraced each other and cried for a little longer. Still no one else reacted. The horror of the loss that hadn't happened that night came over me. Very briefly I imagined living with Papka, with my brother and sisters and no Mama. I needed her so much in my life and it had no meaning without her. Only she knew whether it was I who stopped her from killing herself, a fear of killing herself, or she just couldn't find a way to tie her robe belt on anything stable in there.

My friend, Irmantas, wasn't so lucky. His parent's marriage seemed harmonious and happy. His mother smiled a lot. They lived in a big house, had a car and stable jobs that allowed them to go on a beach holiday every summer. Irmantas was a giant, gentle boy who preferred living with his grandma, Ona, and playing with me, instead of going to school where smaller boys taunted him.

Until one day, according to Ona, he finished his lunch in the school canteen, took his tray back and on the way out went to his bully's table and flung the boy on the floor. Everyone's jaw dropped, including the bully himself. Following his long summer holiday in the village, his parents would come down to pick him up and we, reluctant to part, played every minute away. His mother implored him to go back in and get changed for the journey. He came back to me, and we decided to make an airplane whereby we could escape. With sticks we drew the blueprint of the model on the sand. Together we decided what essential parts it would need to fly. We both sincerely believed in the manifestation of the desire if only wished for enough.

A few planes now and again would pass across the sky over our village, leaving a white streak behind them. Who was on those planes and what country were they going to, I wondered when I lay on my back in the grass, watching them slit the perfect, tranquil sky and follow its path for a while, wondering if they were foreign, rich people. I wondered if they could see everything below them, my village, me. I wondered if they landed, could I just hop on, like on a bus. I had never been to the airport or seen a plane from up close before. If children saw a helicopter hovering above, they would wave and run after it.

Irmantas's mother hanged herself. There was a rumour going around that she had lost her battle with depression. Some years later when he came down again, our magical moments were over. My puberty hormones made me put a supercilious act on and snub him every time we encountered each other on the stairs. Just like a foolish young girl, I wanted him to show interest in me, maybe even a slightly gallant pursuit of my company, but when he wanted to help me to push a heavy cart, I rejected his advances. I'll tell you what it was. It was an empty pride shaped by the sheer embarrassment of being seen performing laborious, provincial jobs with calluses on my hands. He had lived in the city all those years, and just like that decided to pop by to see his grandma, but I was still this little country girl wearing tatty clothes. This was the last time I saw him, and I regretted it.

Despite Irmantas's grandmother's amplified curiosity to know everything, to partake in everything, to jump to impetuous conclusions and to frighten children and adults, she eased my mother's suffering from the perpetual lack of money. Ona had some distant relative who needed a shop assistant in a secondhand clothes store he planned to open in our village. He needed a reliable, presentable, local, communicative female without a drinking habit. He thought my Mama was too old to be a store assistant at forty-two. Ona insisted he wouldn't find better. Mama was advised to put her best clothes on and come meet her prospective employer and his wife. After a few shots of vodka, the man put his hand on Mama's shoulder and asked:

"Well, dear, are we going to work together, what do you think?"

Most people who say that money doesn't bring you happiness only say that because they don't know what unhappiness is. One day Mama came back from her work do slightly tipsy and in a good mood. She sat on my father's lap, and he had his arms around her and they were speaking nicely to each other. I played on the floor with my toys; this really baffled me.

"What is happening?" I pondered "Is he no longer a bad man?"

Chapter VI

Mama proved to be a natural-born saleswoman. She understood the power of live modeling of the clothes to pique people's interest in the stuff she was selling. She would get the first pick of the stock and pay for it from her wages. The clothes were worn but of high quality. There was even a pair of Versace jeans among everything else. Maybe they weren't Versace. Mama couldn't possibly have known that at the time but decades later she insisted that they were. This secondhand clothes concept was very alien in our country hence no surprise that people were hesitant to buy at first. Our educated teacher-neighbours would come to ours to express their amazement at the almost new and perfectly fine duck duvet. The items spoke for themselves and so they started giving Mama the money to bring them something of that same quality from her store. They were teachers, they could not possibly be seen shopping in secondhand places. Since the mandatory school uniforms had been removed, the disparity between pupils' parents' incomes was stark. One day you were going to school in the same outfit as everyone else, the next day you understood that you were poor. Your peers were too quick to notice that. Mama didn't earn a huge amount of money, but one, her children had been clothed, two, she gained a bit of prestige in the village social circles and three, she had more independence from her husband's income.

The shop had a cement floor, no heating, no toilet or water, an electric heater made no difference. I spent most of my last pre-school days in the shop and hassled Mama to sell my grotesque paintings for ten or twenty cents and bigger pictures for fifty cents. I displayed them at the counter but made zero sales. Next door there was a state-run food shop, a notch warmer than ours, with very lovely and jaunty ladies working there. At first Mama enjoyed their company behind the curtain at the back of our shop, where they would keep themselves animated and warm with shots of vodka. Soon she grew weary of it and realised it was not the slippery slope that she wanted to take. The back of the shop behind the curtain brought a lot of joy to friends and new acquaintances alike. Mama made connections with the outdoor market sellers by inviting them for some warmth. In gratitude they held their best products for her for a special price.

Everyone made fun of a short guy and his big, tall missus because of their size differences. They sold bicycle parts and people were shocked to hear that he used to beat her up. Mrs. Leach had the pleasure of being asked for a dance by him in some corporate event one time.

She stifled her laughter when he rubbed himself against her and kept asking if she liked that. Mrs. Leach had a nice petite figure with a curvaceous rear.

As a child I didn't see the value in organic home-grown food and always craved sugary stuff from the shops. I loved the chocolate eggs *Kinder Surprise* and fizzy drinks. Rarely was I bought either of those things, so I thought I was being clever when I nicked two Litas from the till and went to another shop - not the one next door - to buy a bottle of lemonade. If Mama asked where I had got it from, I'd say some woman had given it to me. What a brilliant plan, I thought, and so the moment of execution arrived. We used to go to the well for some water near the decrepit house where two silly boys lived.

They loved calling me racist names whenever they saw me, so I avoided going there on my own. One event put me off: we were walking home from the shop and bypassed one of those silly boys who said to his friend "Look, that's *Chukchi*," and laughed. Mama turned around and retorted with an equally cruel remark pertaining to his blue-faced mother, so that he would feel the same hurt I did, through no fault of his.

While Mama was busy drawing water from the well, I quickly sneaked into the shop, put the money on the counter and asked the lady to give me a big bottle of lemonade. My nervousness must have given me away for she deliberately started asking me probing questions, while looking through the window for my mother. I expected to get punished for stealing the money and lying, but instead Mama bought me lemonade that day. I never stole again, except for some petty change from her purse to pay Felix for doing my maths homework, which resulted in my terrible end-of-year marks.

In the dreary days of the economic breakdown after the Soviet Union dissolved, teachers went through spells of working without pay for six months or more. Mama tasked Varvara to go to the shops and humble herself in front of the shop assistants to give us some bread, flower, pasta, oil, and buckwheat on credit. The rest of the food we grew ourselves. I was too young to do that, Jelena didn't live at home, Felix was a boy. I remember my sister came back in tears once. She had been shamed by this red-nosed, alkie cleaning woman who had called the poor girl out in front of everyone in the shop.

"Tell your mother to pay back what she already owes us first, before coming back here again!" Sadly, for Varvara this experience didn't end there; she had to try other shops and ask for the same list of items, in the hope that she wouldn't encounter hostile staff or any kids from school.

Varvara was not Jelena, but Mama didn't believe that two daughters could be that much different. Varvara didn't do well at school. Even when Mama arranged that her boss's wife would give her some private English lessons for a litre of warm milk a day, Varvara wasn't interested. The only things she liked doing were singing, going out dancing and cutting pictures from styling magazines. Even though she had a nice, melodic voice and quickly established herself as one of the two singers brave enough to perform solo in front of the audience at school, this meant nothing. Art had no place in provincial schools. Music lessons were a forty-five minute gap between your regular subjects to catch up with your homework, or simply muck about with your friends and get a maximum mark by default anyway. In Varvara's case, our married, middle-aged music teacher, locked her in his classroom and confessed his love to her. He wanted to know if she was still a virgin and if she was, he would leave his wife if that was what my sister wanted him to do. If she was still a virgin, he desired to be the one who took her virginity from her. The intimidated teenage girl let him kiss her to get him off her back. She made herself popular singing the famous soundtrack to the film *Titanic* with the lovesick teacher playing the piano in the background. Mama didn't approve of her singing; this was supposed to be an after-lessons activity and was by no means to be taken seriously. Our mother herself played the accordion and had a beautiful voice. One night she was woken up by my granddad, who told his tipsy friends "And now, my daughter will play Bach," and she did as she was told. Mama never had any faith in her children and because we looked different to everyone else around there, she had dinned into us that our only way out was to study hard and work hard. She told us that because of the way we looked, our lives would be more challenging, and we would need to try twice as hard.

Unlike Jelena, Varvara had friends and didn't show much enthusiasm for work either. She cleaned and cooked, baked cakes and made the best homemade ice cream, and if she had the chance to get out of working on an endless mangold field, she would rather take that chance. She wanted to own many nice clothes and beauty products like she saw her city friends and the Leach girls do, but her natural beauty attracted the attention of many boys and grown-up men alike without the help of accessories. She was hugely embarrassed by an athletic, married, and what seemed at that time, old thirty something man, whose daughter she occasionally baby sat. They moved back to the city shortly after.

Varvara said she couldn't understand why he was paying her that sort of attention when his wife was a very pretty and slim woman. Even if you're a young teenage girl, you'd rather receive your compliments from someone like that than your mother's friend's sleazy husband, who leered at you and tested your modesty with indecent remarks. Such a man was Mr. Luktuk. This vulgar man spoke about girls' underwear and figures in the most lurid way. Drunk or sober, there wasn't a significant difference in his conduct: he always scolded his wife, called her a whore, and threatened to kill her while obsessively following her everywhere she went, more so when drunk. She had to hide under Mama's bed, maybe more than once. He was up to date with the village gossip, which he was partially responsible for and splashed his wages entirely in one evening, or weekend if he stopped by Laura's parents, who hosted him for as long as his money lasted. He was greedy and had a chip on his shoulder because all his brothers and sisters had done well for themselves, so he went around the village boasting how powerful his family was. Varvara loathed Mr. Luktuk. So did Mama, but Mrs. Luktuk was a lovely lady who never refused us anything. She secretly sent us a bag of flour when I was small and we really needed it, without her husband's knowledge.

When the husbands of these wives failed to provide for their families, they'd cooperate among themselves by trading food and vegetables.

Mr. and Mrs. Shmickle were a lovely couple, who always seemed so deeply in love with each other.

They were the youngest of our family friends. Mr. Shmickle was a born fisherman and if he was successful that day, he'd share his fish with us. Those two were also a little bit more naive. Briefly, very briefly, someone gave us their posh dog, not a mongrel, but a big, tall, perpetually salivating, large-jawed dog. We simply named him 'Dog'. Those people couldn't have thought of a better place to dump their unwanted dog. Mama was a big animal lover and couldn't say no. They got rid of him because he was a thick and insatiable creature. Personally, I felt it was unfair that this spoilt dog stayed indoors with us, while my poor Rubik had to live in a kennel, and I was only too happy when Mama convinced Mrs. Shmickle to take him for free. Those days when I didn't go to the shop with Mama, I had to take Dog out for walks in winter and my child's weight was not enough to keep hold of him. He'd pull the leash so hard that my palms hurt until I had to let go of it, then lose my breath running after him, as if I had nothing better to do. My dolls needed mothering and home building, drawing skills had to be honed to produce quality pictures for Mama's shop, and patients needed to be revived and cured of illnesses.

"You have a big house, loads of room," Mama said to her friend. Not only did that bugger swallowed anything edible and non-edible in his massive gob, but he also opened the doors to the living room, where the party was happening, and demonically sat and stared at people eating, oozing long trails of saliva. His greed was what killed him. Not long after he moved to his new home, he began devouring chickens, so they had to shoot him.

Mama was popular with people before she even started working in the shop. We'd always have someone stopping by, or some of the closest family friends gathering for some party and music. After a few drinks, my mother's Slavic soul would get the better of her, she'd pull out her Russian shawl and start dancing and singing. She loved it when people listened to her talking about my grandfather's war experience, exactly as I do today - I suppose there is a bit of Mr. Luktuk in all of us. Those rare moments will always be remembered by me as some of my mother's happiest ones. But there will also be those opaque episodes of her playing dramatic Russian songs in the dark living room alone. Time and again, I watched cheesy Russian gangsters in leather jackets dancing drunk to very similar songs in films about the *Wild Nineties*. Gangs in the nineties in Eastern Europe were a destructive threat to many people, but in films, throw in a romance line and give them a noble cause, they'd win your heart. Was Mama sad when she listened to her songs alone in the dark?

Was she feeling nostalgic? Homesick? Emotional? Was she pondering how her life would have turned out had she chosen a dashing German suitor instead of my father? Once in a bitter emotional state, she said if she had, she would have lived like a queen in a castle in Germany - but she was certainly the queen of the party. People were drawn to my mother, but my father didn't make any friends and was a man of few words. At parties he'd just sit silent, stuff his face, and whenever his favourite singer came on, he'd make a solemn face, purse his lips and mutter "Sad song. Sad song."

Mother didn't approve of this singer "One trick pony," she used to say. She was right. This sad song was a hit of the nineties in Russian speaking countries and likely on a gangsters' party play list as well. Not to come across as being condescending to Russian pop artists, Gary Moore's *Parisienne Walkaway*, a big favourite of my mother's too, was even more often chosen by leather-jacketed thugs to release suppressed human emotions, owing to its prolonged bluesy guitar chords. How I wanted to have a big party just like Greta Leach's Christening celebration. The Leaches threw a feast in their youngest's honour - they needed to borrow a long table to serve the jam-packed living room. She wore a beautiful white dress and acquired Godparents, she even stood up for me that day. I was the only girl wearing a white shirt underneath a grey pinafore, my upcoming September the First outfit. Her cheeky cousin said to us that because I was not wearing a dress like those two, I ought to be their servant and they would be princesses. Greta snapped and told her to stop talking rubbish, the dim cousin seemed abashed. When everyone got drunk and I was no longer there, but at home in bed and just sharing what everyone talked about the following day, Mr. Leach instructed his wife to put on her new real leather jacket and give their guests a show. The philandering husband of another neighbour asked the women if they had ever seen a male striptease before, they giggled, when he asked if they would like to see it- hey giggled, but egged him on. He started gyrating and told Mrs. Leach to pull the belt off his trousers. She, of course, burst into laughter, the male stripper's dreams were crushed when his wife punched him hard enough to land him on the floor. Everyone laughed. She was much smaller than him, but a violent person and often threw things at him at home. My awkward father, suffering from a terrible hangover, put on his suit the next morning and went back to the Leaches in the hope of being offered a remedy, but they didn't let him in.

What I didn't understand was why Mama would keep beautiful, little white dresses in her wardrobe for me, but wouldn't allow me to wear them. It was for my Christening, Jelena used to say to me. Naturally, I would confront her with the obvious need to know when that would take place, and who would my Godparents be, but I got my dreams shattered by yet another outgrown beautiful dress which was later sold for someone else's daughter's Christening. We had a church, a dress, potential Godparents, so why did I have to wait and wait for another next thing to happen before that?

It's almost as if most of my childhood was plagued by the necessary order of things to occur before I could have what had been promised. This entrenched the habit of passively waiting for external circumstances to improve in my life, before I could act of my own accord, and almost infinite patience in dull jobs in years to come. That first thing that needed to happen in my case was of course, the right church, which was the Orthodox Christian church. I cannot say that my mother was remotely religious at that point in her life. There was a very old icon of Christ on the wall in front of which she prayed. The rest of us didn't know how to, nor did we know anything about religion or how the faith of the locals differed to that of our mother's. We knew that Papka was supposed to be Muslim, but we never witnessed him following his belief either.

People in our village didn't know better either. My ditsy history teacher embarrassed me in front of my whole class when she said that; "There is one person in this class who could have been an adherent of Islam today, because her father is a Muslim". I guess her aim was to emphasise diversity. A perfectly decent boy at the back of the room shouted out to me; "Is your father a terrorist then?" The teacher's face was blank, which made me realise that I was alone against everyone here, so I retorted something back to defend my father's reputation. A terrorist? Give me a break. I yearn to know what makes perfectly decent boys spout inanities like that, more often than is needed. None of this religious stuff meant anything to me, other than that being baptised brought you closer to God and this was what every girl I knew wanted. The next big deal was your First Communion, but I wouldn't ever have that pleasure because it is a Catholic ceremony and we were not, I was told, before my fantasies of my own Christening party carried me away. We were nothing really, there was just this aspiration fostered by our Mama to keep us as close to her roots as possible. We were going to become and belong where she saw us, but later, each one of us on our terms. What she wanted was to have us all baptised in a church in Kaliningrad. Then there comes a second thing that needed to happen - having the financial means to take us there.

First Felix, then I, had to aid and abet mother in lying to the bus driver that we were younger than we truly were, so we could travel on a reduced child's fare. Not that the drivers gave that much of a damn, it's just that we sometimes forgot what the agreed narrative was and almost divulged our real age.

"How old are you, child?"

"Seven."

"Five!" Mama would correct me.

"No Mama, I'm seven." How dare she diminish my maturity? Unspeakable.

"I thought your mum said you're five?" The cheeky driver was out to catch one of us being insincere.

"Nastassja, you're five, remember?" There was no way Mama was paying more than she could get away with. No parent would.

You were a laughing-stock if you did.

"I forgot. I'm five." I remembered. No more questions asked.

Mama didn't like taking Varvara to Kaliningrad to see Grandpa Alexey. It used to be Felix, Jelena and I who were bestowed those scant trips that my sister envied. Varvara disliked it when the Luktuks visited us, especially when that caricature of a man chaperoned his wife.

Mama didn't relish his company either, but his electrician's skills were very valuable and came at mate's rates. As Mama put it, she was forever in debt to them for not letting her children die of starvation, a little bit of an exaggeration, but true nevertheless. I don't think Papka liked him either and Varvara's reporting on his visits only compounded his jealousy. This caused arguments. The same jealousy was the reason why mother didn't defend her dissertation and failed to obtain a formal higher education. This did not prevent her from getting work and even managing other people under her, but in the world outside the West, where education was esteemed over natural aptitude, my mother regularly found herself relegated to the lower ranks. She loved emphasising the power of the academic degree.

"If you have a paper to prove you have graduated from something, you are a human being. If you don't have a paper to prove that you graduated from something, you are not a human being."

Papka was so jealous of his wife that he insisted on coming with Mama and Mrs. Leach for their late-night swims in the river. Mama was so poor she couldn't afford a swimming suit, so she had to wait for the sun to set and everyone to clear off to be able to swim. Mrs. Leach had a swimming suit.

Papka caused a lot of grief to Mama, and this brought a hefty amount of unhappiness to us children. There are fewer things in our lives in this world that hurt us more than seeing our mothers unhappy. I remember a deep sense of discomfort seeing my parents push each other, causing things to fall on the floor. I found myself trying to break up their grappling by getting in between them and shrieking along. I always tried to release Papka's grip on Mama, I kicked him and hit him. And I watched the hurt and disbelief in his eyes when I called him offensive names, exactly the same names that would hurt me too because they were intended to scorn his ethnicity. Those intense brown eyes of a defensive animal either belonged to my father or a demon inside him. Mama hardly ever succumbed to father's efforts to intimidate her with his protruding jaw, blue lips and his habit of spouting saliva in her face. The few times she put her hand on his face and averted it as far away as she could, Papka hit her. As a martial arts enthusiast, he enthusiastically practised the moves on her. He aimed at the joints on her legs and arms; those delicate bones that hurt like hell if you hit yourself on the sharp end of your bed.

Mama aimed at pulling his hair, which worked like kryptonite each time. The whole house and the street heard those fights, and sometimes neighbours would get involved. f so, Papka became silent and acted as if nothing had happened, or said that it was Mama's fault and she had provoked the fight. One time, when he was getting ready to leave after the payday weekend visiting us, he got on mother's nerves by pestering her about a pair of shoes that he couldn't fit into. She wrenched off the whole section of the wardrobe where all the shoes were stored and scattered it across the whole room, then went to the bedroom and didn't come out until he had left. Papka sputtered words like "hysteric" and "erratic", put his coat and a black hat on, took his battered, green sports bag with clean clothes and home-produced food and made his way to the bus stop.

Another frightening memory of mine was when Mama lay on the floor by the door and cried. She refused to get up and looked like she had given up on life. I sat by her side in tears and begged her to get up. One of my siblings went down to get Mrs. Leach, but when she came over, she smiled and thought the sight was funny. She asked us to get a sheet to cover Mama. This went on for a bit longer before Mama rose to her feet and went to bed, but Mrs. Leach seemed amused the whole time and eager to go home.

Hate and hurt enabled Mama to burn the letters of her husband's relatives from Kazakhstan. She was revolted that those folks never offered any palpable help to us when we could have done with some. They didn't come to the wedding, nor did they offer a present in any form other than a long list of name suggestions for Jelena. The story circulated in our family about the time when Papka called his father to announce his wedding, and asked for some money to cover the costs.

"Dad, I'm getting married."

"Excellent news, my son. Congratulations to you both."

"Thank you. Dad, I was wondering if you could send me some money, I need to pay for some things."

"What's that? I didn't catch that, my son."

"I said, would it be possible for you to send me some money to help me out with the wedding expenses?"

"I can't hear you." Papka repeated himself several more times, but his old man kept saying; "I cannot hear you." He never asked for anything again. My other granddad paid for everything, but he loved rubbing that in Mama's face and teased her with questions about when her husband's family would endorse them with any financial support.

Besides the money, Papka's folks penned a lot of nonsensical advice in those letters, according to Mama, who read them before she burnt them. They employed a very pompous writing style, and they were encouraging him to move to Kazakhstan with the whole family and reminding him that a wife was meant to be subdued and aware of her wifely duties.

Hurt made our embittered Mama say cruel things to Varvara, as dad's staunch informer. It's true that Mama was sometimes cruel to all her daughters, but she distinguished her second daughter as the least attractive one: with her eyes too far from each other like a goat's, a nose too wide, hunch-backed like a cat, and overall, the one that resembled her father the most. Sadly, my oldest sister Jelena took out her ordinarily well-managed anger on her too by making fun of Varvara's early puberty, calling her a fat cow, which she wasn't, and remorselessly beating her in front of her friends when she refused to go home. Jelena disliked all her sisters' friends and despised them for having those friends. Not one of us has been left untouched by the good and bad infusions of our parents.

It wasn't the Jelena that I knew. My Jelena sent me postcards with Moomins from Finland and bought me a cute pink backpack for school, which was also of a superior quality, which aggravated me in later years because I wanted to change it to a black, feminine handbag like other girls my age, but the backpack was still in good nick. She bought me a light green tracksuit, which no one else had, trainers, and the loveliest pair of black sandals with red flowers embroidered on the wedges. Our dress and shoe sizes intersected at one point in my adolescence when those shoes became too small for me but perfect for her. I was all set up for school that summer; I couldn't wait to go to school!

That was the first summer Jelena spent labouring on a Finnish farm and earning the money which she poured into our household. She bought us a microwave, a washing machine, and a large sofa for the living room. The only two things she rewarded herself with were paying for her driving license and a Hi-Fi which was more for Felix really. Whenever she came back from university, she'd bring a new CD with her. For someone who played the piano and sang in her university choir, Jelena's taste in music was somewhat limited. One of her frequent choices was *Ace of Base*. Now, it's unfair of me to make such statements; there was a period in my life when I thought they were a legitimate band. Jelena grew up in the Soviet Union, she had a lot of catching up to do, but this required resources and effort, and that was not something she was going to direct her focus on. Early one August morning, I was woken up by my sister's gentle tickle only to envelope her in hugs and kisses. I loved Mama and Jelena the most, Felix and Varvara were not interested in me anymore.

The three of us traveled to Kaliningrad by train and slept on a couch at Baba Toma's. She had only one grandson and two daughters, of whom she was immensely proud because they held degrees and had careers. This pride compensated for their lack of visits. Baba Toma was an exuberant and a scary woman to me. It was no surprise when they left me with her for a few hours and went to see my uncle and grandfather. I was overcome with intense sadness and began oozing tears. I was under the impression that they had left me there and had gone back home without me. Suddenly, the idea of spending the entire summer away from home with Baba Toma didn't appeal to me in the slightest. My tantrum forced her to finally dress me up and walk me to where she said my mother and sister were, for I had to see for myself that they hadn't abandoned me. The minute we left the house, we bumped into them - I felt safe and happy again.

Baba Toma was kind, loud, big, fair, self-assured, and believed there was nothing more supreme than celestial justice. She was verbally expressive and inventive, and she readily reminded people of their hypocrisy and shortcomings. She embodied the soul of the common Russian folk.

One time, someone gave me a type of chocolate that I had never seen before - a long chocolate bar. Out of gluttony and excitement I almost devoured it at once, Baba Toma walked into the room and snatched it away from me.

"What a rascal, shovelling in the whole bar of chocolate! Give it here immediately!" she placed it on the top of the cupboard, supposedly out of my reach. I saw where she had placed it and I managed to get to it by climbing onto the stool, but I didn't dare to touch it. There is one thing that has been on my conscience and will remain there until the day I die and meet all my deceased relatives and will be able to tell her I'm sorry. Telling myself that I was just a stupid child, and she most likely knew it when I uttered this rude and thick remark to her, doesn't make the shame go away. My Baba Toma used to dry pumpkin seeds on her windowsills and snack on them when watching TV. She and I were busying ourselves with just that by an open window to her little garden, which needed pruning, but as her daughters lived in mainland Russia and weren't there to take care of such things, the poor woman did what she could. The conversation between us was going somewhere because she lowered herself to my level of emotional immaturity but rose back up again when I said this.

"I can spit really far," I said.

"Oh, can you? Good for you". These may not be her exact words, but what else can you say to such a silly remark?

"I can spit on you if you want me to...?"

"Why would you spit on me? For my hospitality to your family? For the bed and food, I share with you. Why would you do such a thing to me?" I wanted to tell her it was a joke. I never meant to spit on her, I just thought it was funny and she'd laugh at it. It was something that I would have said to my friends back home and it would have passed as funny banter, and no one would have got offended. I meant no harm, no disrespect, I was just a crass, uneducated, provincial child who hung out with other dim, unsophisticated children like me. I didn't apologise. I went into my shell like a snail or a turtle, which I did whenever someone yelled at me or called me out for my behaviour.

Chapter VII

Why is it that we, as adults, still want to cringe when remembering some silly things that we did or said when we were very young? I was a gullible, sensitive but wicked girl and got into situations that the Leach girls would never have. That thing that I do, retracting back to my shell when something like that happens, I still do today, and it must be for a good reason that life keeps presenting me with such circumstances so I can rectify my character. But I know I won't - it's easier to be in a shell than do anything else.

Gossiping about your family friends is a common occurrence in most families, and I hope I'm right about it, but it shouldn't be done in front of the children. Our home was too crowded and I'm truly amazed looking back, how on earth we all fit into the twenty-five-square-meter flat. As much as Mama admired the Leach family for their family dynamics and a distinctive motivation to work themselves flat out, which allowed them to own the latest of everything, she also expressed her sour criticism of such things like Mrs. Leach being skinny as a plank, their messy home or their not so salubrious beginnings. Mama often liked to drop little pieces of knowledge about the latter to motivate us even more - you see, even someone like that can pull themselves up by their own bootstraps. The part that got me into trouble was the new hair colour of their middle daughter - it was a yellowy-blond colour explicitly achieved if dyed at home.

My Mama didn't approve of it and used some similes to make her point.

Because I didn't share the Leach's genes, I went off and repeated all that to other girls who I thought were my friends. The Leach girls would not have done such a stupid thing. The whole block of girls ganged up on me.

They lured me into their playground area where the girl with yellow hair was waiting for me to redress the insult.

"Nastassja, I've been told you don't like my hair colour?" I was gobsmacked. She was friends with Varvara, why was she being a dick to me?

"I didn't say that." I tried to defend myself. I had no allies. I looked around me, they were all traitors. Back to the shell.

"You did! You did!" That Princess - it was her who I had said this to, in confidence of course. So when I confided in her, she must have been twitching as if she had a firecracker in her arse the entire time, dying to shoot off as fast as she could to report on me to the Leach girls. "You also said that her mum was scrawny!" I did say those things, but it made no difference whether I admitted it or not now several sets of fiendish eyes were relishing the gratification derived from mob justice. Oh, so what, I bet they were saying meaner things about my family! At least I gave those children, devoid of any human decency, an excitement that I bet no one has ever had the guts to do since. I kept looking down and said nothing. The Leach sister received no apology from me and started to make derogatory racial slurs. My legs were rooted to the ground. There was nothing holding me there, but I still couldn't move. It's odd how I managed to reconcile myself to every ounce of racist ridicule addressed to me. I told myself; "Let them say whatever they have got to say to me, they will give up shortly, because I'm not reacting." Then I heard my mother's voice exploding from our house patio.

"What did you say to her?! Look at you, a giant mare with tits accosting a little child! Have you no shame?!" Nastassja, you come home this instance!" That voice saved me. No one dared to retort to my mother. I went home, and they all went into hiding.

The rift didn't last long between those girls and me. Very soon, if not the next day, we were playing together again. Falling out and forming allegiances was a common occurrence among us, so was gossiping about one another, sealed by extracting a promise that this would only remain between the teller and the listener. At the time, Ausra was a member of the other group, so when she turned up at my playground where a friend and I had built a lovely home for our thriving imaginary families, we were very suspicious. Ausra was sad and looking to join our group because she had had an argument with the others and left them. My credulity led me straight into the trap she had set for me. We kindly welcomed her to our home, which we were so proud of, only to find it all ransacked and knocked down. My partner and I decided that Ausra had been sent as a spy. We tidied up, I repotted my smashed plant pots, and we continued playing, leaving the incident behind us. After all we would probably be friends with her in no time. We never found out if the spy theory was plausible, though come to think of it now, Ausra did have a few screws loose in that ginger head of hers, literally.

Foraging was one of our favourite ways of having some downtime in the summer.. In the village there was an abundance of apples, pears and berries, which when consumed too often and in immoderate amounts caused us to run to the bushes more often than usual. There was no way that one of us locals would run home to use the toilet and wash our hands like the city kids. Wild strawberry picking season was everyone's most awaited time because it was the shortest, the berries were the tastiest and if someone was too slow, they didn't get to pierce them nicely on the dry grass stem and walk around with the trophy evoking jealousy in their peers. Trends came and went quickly, like my friend Evie and her evil twin Princess, who shared their discovery of edible grass roots. They were edible, but they might have been the cause of the dreadful appendicitis that befell me just a couple of years down the line. The abundance of natural vitamins right in the hub of our communal childhood was a blessing for those children who didn't often get fed at home by their alcoholic parents.

Some of them, like that irksome Brigita, purposefully hung around the city kids, for they knew that the grandmothers of those kids would bring out some treats to be shared with them. The city kids also held no prejudice against them, which must have been a relief. Lice, on the other hand, was not something they could prevent, and God help you if you were identified as the unfortunate, lice-ridden wretch at school who had infected the whole class. And believe me, the nurse at school made sure that you would get identified and shamed. The most likely outcome that you could expect was the taunts and jeers of everyone who knew you, and even those who were new to school, because your reputation preceded you swiftly. The school authorities alerted the parents accordingly, but if yours were more bothered to know where their next bottle was coming from, you only had yourself to count on.

A few girls I mixed with in my pre-school days had lice, but I only realised this when Jelena took me to Kaliningrad for a weekend. At the train station, we went to a nice coffee shop with funky chairs and ambient lighting, where she bought me a cup of tea and a donut. I devoured the treat and asked her if I could get another one, got no reply, then asked one more time, still no reply and no donut. This was my first time in a coffee shop, my first time trying a donut and the first time being surrounded by people I had never encountered before - I was in a city. The day after we arrived, my persistent head scratching got noticed by my aunt, who together with Jelena, stayed up all night picking the lice out of my long hair. My benign aunt seemed to own a patience of gold, and that's the only memory I have held of her ever since - leaning over and ridding me of my embarrassing predicament while keeping a cheerful countenance. In all honesty, I didn't feel embarrassed, but my sister did, while my dear uncle sat in the kitchen and murmured reproaches that added to Jelena's discomfort.

"What sort of lousy relatives do I have? Coming to my house, passing their scummy lice on." Luckily, the danger of this succession was contained at the right time, leaving my uncle's household unaffected.

However exuberant the games and adventures were with friends of my own age, I jumped at every meager opportunity to tag along with the friends of my siblings. Greta Leach's sisters didn't mind her following them, which conferred some sort of age prestige on her - I suppose it has always been universally perceived as a level up if you are accepted by the peers of your older siblings. Greta didn't snitch on her sisters like I did when Varvara sat on her boyfriend's lap. I told Mama and she forbade Varvara to see that boy again, but how effective is precluding a teenager from following the direction in which the butterflies in their stomach desire to go?

Mama stood in her way with her arms crossed when my sister tried to leave for the disco, with her hair adorably curled from keeping it in many little braids for days to achieve this effect. Varvara's friend from the city plaited her hair while I sycophantically admired her good looks. She was a lanky girl with thin blond hair and a plain face that seemed very attractive to a very young mind. She seemed to love wearing dungarees, checked shirts, denim shorts and crop tops. Girls in our village didn't dare to dress like that. The girl's name was my namesake - I somewhat felt that she owed me friendship, so I pestered her to paint my nails a light blue colour like hers. It was more like asking her to fix the damage I had already caused to my nails. I had daubed the nail varnish beyond my nail borders. If I remember rightly, they also had dirt underneath them. She picked up my plump little hand, looked at it and said; "Next time start at your knuckles" and dropped it. I don't think she liked me very much. Mama had a problem with Varvara being friends with that outlandish girl and she couldn't have embarrassed her more than scathingly voicing her thoughts aloud in her friend's earshot.

"She looks like she swallowed a pole. She is not a friend for you, that long-legged wench!" she also mentioned her Lithuanised German surname and her well-off father. "She's only using you to amuse herself for the season, do you think she would ever hang out with you outside this village?" Mama was a good person and a strict parent, but she channeled some of the sourest qualities when her short temper called her to do so, and she wasn't always a model of punctiliousness.

The next morning, the girl said to Varvara; "I know your mother doesn't approve of our friendship. Last night, I stood beneath your balcony and heard her saying those things about me and my family, I understand Russian". How do you respond, how do you defend your mother in a situation like that? None of this tainted their friendship. Mama was wrong: the long-legged wench didn't corrupt her daughter's soul for she indeed was a person of substance. However, she permanently set the ideal body standard for a perfectly healthy teenager. When my namesake came by to see my sister one time, Varvara was making herself sick in the toilet.

"Your friend came looking for you, I called you, but you didn't respond," I said. It was strange to me, because in summer, your city friends take priority over everyone and everything else, so when they do grace you with their presence at your door, you run to them, which was what Varvara had always done. And I did too.

"I was in the toilet, what did you want me to do?" she was lying.

"I heard you vomiting," I stuck to my guns.

"You're wrong, I was sitting on the toilet!"

"I'm going to tell mum that you vomited."

Mother's reaction was what all of us feared in our family, everyone except Felix. Varvara went for different tactics.

"Nastassja, I think you and I should get healthy this summer and start working out. What do you say?"

"Yeah, we can do that," I was signing up for something I hadn't a clue about.

"But the thing is, our exercise routine must be followed with a good diet."

"Is our diet not good?" We spoke as we laid in our bunk bed late in the evening. After Jelena left, we got rid of my cot bed, which was too poky for me anyway. A few front bars had to be broken and removed to facilitate my climbing in and out of it - I did break them, of course! I was given Felix's bottom bed and he moved to the couch in the living room. The new sleeping arrangements were coming in shortly - the corner sofa bed that Jelena bought us permitted all three of us to sleep in one room, giving Mama the space in the bedroom.

"The food we eat is fattening, it's all potatoes, pork and pasta." said Varvara, "How about whenever Mama goes to town, let's ask her to buy us fruit juice, bananas and oranges, instead of sweets and chocolates?"

"Okay." The thought of swapping already rare treats for bloody fruits deeply saddened me and no sooner had I assured my sister I'd follow through with this agreement, than I began hatching a plan to wriggle out of it. Maybe, I reckoned, I would ask Mama to continue bringing me chocolates and sweets, while Varvara could have bananas? I was seven years old and had just been manipulated into thinking that I needed body enhancement by dieting and exercising. Either way, I was utterly useless in any of my sister's schemes, but Felix proved to be otherwise.

Everyone always said that boys mature later and are not as interested in relationships as the girls would like them to be. At thirteen, my brother looked no further than his immediate circle of associates to pledge his first commitment to a girl, who looked like a boy. Come to think of it now, because of her thick, dark eyebrows she looked somewhat more boyish. She happened to be the younger sister of Varvara's boyfriend. It's a pity that the match didn't last - the girl grew up to become an attractive, educated, and ambitious woman - my brother's loss. With Mama becoming increasingly alarmed over the alliance forming between her daughter and the city boy, she resorted to pretty harsh measures to put an end to it. If the revelation of the boy's distant, disgraced uncle didn't put Varvara off him, then surely chasing him around the plum tree at night would put him off her.

Most Friday nights my brother and sister went out to the village disco. He wasn't interested in that sort of thing yet, but she implicated him to appease our anxious mother. Mama would wait for them to come back until the very early morning hours, when she had made it clear the curfew hour was eleven. Making out with the one you desired on the dingy dance-floor to the pop tunes that would always bring back those memories, was worth surrendering to the ruthless punishment you would have to endure later. I would also remember those songs as I lay in my bed listening, unable to imagine why anyone would want to be out there at this time. We lived five minutes from the Community Centre and the school.

You ring the doorbell and listen to the sound of her footsteps, the click of the light switch, the turn in the keyhole, and her scowling face appearing to pierce your conscience, but you don't have any, instead you give her the puppy eyes in a hope that maybe she will just let you pass through the threshold safely this time. She steps back just enough for you to slide through. Your voice of self-preservation niggles; 'Don't do it.' Think of the highlights of the night, of how besotted you are with that boy and his warm mouth on yours, while you're being wiped the floor with, hurled by your tousled hair. It's impossible to do both - to push back her hands off your blameless scalp and evade the blows of the cord of the plug. There is so much to live for, so much to look forward to in the life that's barely started for you, but not once has the defeatist thought crossed your mind that maybe he is not worth your writhing in agony every Friday night or ever. The most painful thing that landed on Felix's back was a slipper, even when he wound the clock back by two hours to trick Mama. It took some ingenious skills besides diplomacy to navigate the dynamics between your sister and the mother. He nicked the spare key to let themselves in silently, but Mama kept her key in the lock.

There was no chance of bypassing the gatekeeper. The only time his efforts paid off was when he came back home a bit earlier and left the door unlocked for Varvara.

No one could have predicted the clamorous youth stumbling across the incensed parent at night outside our house: The cocky city boy got to circuit the plum tree abandoning his former swag and chivalry to run away from the mad mother of his girlfriend. Mama threatened 'to show that wormy creep.' The nightly escapade wasn't what eventually broke this concord. He broke up with my sister the next summer when he told her that he was joining the Police Academy, and she was still at school.

Mama's vigour had waned too for the time being. On the summer solstice, a celebration of enormous significance in rural Lithuania, Mama had the milk buckets ready for the refractory pair, so when they entered the house at five in the morning, she sent them off to the pastures to milk the cows.

There was no scolding and hair pulling this time.

Felix wrapped the chain over May's horns to discourage her from kicking Varvara with her back leg, and Varvara cautiously emptied the cow's full udder of milk into the bucket between its legs. It took them ages to milk both cows.

Chapter VIII

Why I had developed the habit of self-aggrandizement from a young age, perhaps could be linked to my need to deflect the spiteful racist name-calling from some stupid children. Mama told me the best way to respond was to say, "So what if I am Chukchi, at least I can read, I can write and speak three languages." Only half of this statement being false, triggered a blatant indignation in my abusers. A glitch in their cognition obstructed their further advances of attack. Since I could read and write and maybe do basic maths before I started school, I was told by everyone, including Mama, that I would be ahead of everyone else and could probably even skip a year. Self-assured, I awaited my auspicious start and engaged in solitary games in the last weeks of August. I sort of had an idea who else was starting school the same year and knew that Brigita was one of them. She stood across the fence and obstinately watched me play until at last, I asked her if she would care to join me.

Almost instantly Brigita won my sympathy: she was gentle, didn't contradict my ideas of how we should proceed with things, and needed my friendship more than I needed hers. She looked as if I had bestowed huge happiness on her by deigning to play with her anywhere else but my garden. She knelt and did my shoelaces sometimes too.

The games we played fired our imaginations and we found the answer to the question of who we wanted to be when we grew up - both of us wanted to perform for the camera and be on television. We took turns in sharing what banal, low budget Lithuanian pop music videos we saw on a Sunday song request TV program aimed at old people. We recreated those videos with us in them, each adding a personal touch and performing in front of each other, describing what costumes we were wearing, what our stage names were and creating the whole universe where our alter egos thrived in the spotlight. When we didn't sing, we acted in our own soap operas based on Latin telenovelas aired at the time. Here we agreed that if one of us was the main female lead in one show, the other one could not be her - she had to pick another one.

Often, we competed about whose character was better looking and went through more dramatic events. This gradually led to a Hollywood star obsession. There was a weekly film and TV magazine that neither of our families subscribed to. The only people who did were my esteemed teacher-neighbours. She and I stole to their door and quickly skimmed through the glamorous pictures before they discovered their post. Brigita had no hesitation when it came to asking other people for things. A precipitous habit that can unconsciously grow into a self-entitled privilege that the world owes you because you're the victim. But Brigita wasn't a victim - she was smart and sometimes she just played the victim card to gain an advantage. My new friend cajoled the chauvinist couple into giving their old magazines to her. I sourced my own celebrity pictures from the redundant popular press from *makulatura* houses that Papka brought from Vilnius. I cut out the pictures and glued them into the old exercise books that I found at home.

What really pushed my buttons was Brigita's flagrant lies about the stuff she claimed she had done or eaten, or the distant, pretty, female cousins she had. If I said to her that I had this television channel that only showed English speaking music videos, she said she had the same. I knew she didn't. I knew she only had four terrestrial channels like everyone else, except a small minority of the neighbours in my house, who had satellite TV. I made up the name of the channel just to see how far she was ready to go to impress me, and it only frustrated me. Her acquiescence to my wrath went along with her constant search for my approval. So great was her determination to keep me as her friend that she even pitted me against my other two friends - Irmantas and Rasa. Watching too many soap operas can be bad for anyone, especially for an impressionable child who soon developed a penchant for poetry and overly dramatic delivery of the lines, in spite of everyone saying that the child was inept at both. Nobody gave out medals just for trying. She told me that Rasa divulged her real motives to her which merely entailed 'wrapping me around her pinky.' Oh, my indignation when she told me this was through the roof. Rasa's aunt and my Papka got involved trying to get to the bottom of this intrigue, but it was to no avail, I stood firm on my decision not to include little Rasa in my games for the time being. The look her chauvinist aunt gave me when I repeated the 'little pinky' line haunted me into my adult years.

There was nothing wrong with Irmantas's toes, but Brigita didn't stop laughing when he opened the door for us barefoot. I chimed in the laughter and mockery of his apparently abnormally crooked toes, although I wouldn't have spotted them and even if I had, I didn't care. Very soon Mama, Irmantas's grandma and Rasa's aunt expressed their discontent with Brigita's meddling in our friendships.

The day was closing in, and I told Brigita that it was time for me to go home. She asked me not to go yet. I felt obliged to stay out a bit longer, but the thing was, I was hungry, and the warmth of my home beckoned me. I missed Mama and my siblings, I wanted to watch a bit of TV too. I asked her if she didn't also want to go home to her family. She pressed her thumb to her lips, as she sometimes did.

"It's cold in my home," she uttered with the utmost sadness. This made me want to run back to my house even more. There was no way that Mama would ever have allowed me to bring her home - we already had to play out of her sight for she forbade me to see Brigita. Besides, I wanted a break from her.

School made our friendship more complicated.

I wore my grey pinafore, a crisp white shirt, my new maroon patent leather shoes with bows, and had my hair voluminously curled. If I had lived a different life, I am sure I could have been a child model - a top cutie like me. On the first of September, Mama and Jelena took me to school and snapped some nice pictures of me. Fortunately, those pictures didn't happen to be the pre-developed film that I laid my hands on and irreversibly ruined. My sister, Jelena, was a lot more forgiving to me back then. To the dismay of every parent of my classmates, we were placed in the hands of the new ingenue teacher from the city. She was a sweetheart, but it only rubbed it in that we had all been simply discarded as a bunch of undesirables by the teacher of the parallel class A. There were thirteen of us in class B.

The bane of our teacher's life was her thinning blond hair and us.

We were an unruly bunch palmed off on her and she relentlessly endeavoured to edify us. She had a good heart, she was sweet, and most importantly she held no prejudice against any of us. She was our pride and we adored her. We even openly made fun of our fellow students in the parallel class - we have a young and beautiful teacher from the city, you're stuck with a brick-faced old woman. The school liked putting up young female teachers in the rooms at the back of the building.

Sometimes after the lessons, a few of us would go to hers with a bouquet of handpicked wild flowers because she gave us sweets, Brigita's idea, of course. We had to leave the flowers at her door the last few visits - the hospitality of your host ought not to be exhausted. Towards the end of our primary school years, the angry tongues of the older, filthy boys spread rumours that our teacher received them in her room. Even my brother dropped hints that my teacher had a side that we didn't know about, but knowing him, it was probably exaggerated nonsense. Felix often talked a lot of rubbish solely to tease me, but over the years, I began to suspect that he derived a lot of pleasure from being able to let down his guard around me and I learned to take most things he said with a pinch of salt.

Did the school turn out to be everything I had hoped for? Actually, besides my exceptionally articulate reading that made the whole class still and silent when I read, I didn't do well at all. My initial self-assurance was short-lived, and I soon drifted into the lower tier of students in my class.

Maths really confused me, and I found it difficult to sustain my focus. My nose was constantly running, and I wiped my boogers onto my black sweater sleeves. I wore the same set of clothes every day - which was the case with pretty much everyone in my class, we were a group with no or very low-income parents - except Meda who changed her outfits frequently. Meda showed greater care for her looks than any other girl her age.

Raised by a single mother, she showed more restraint in her speech and behaviour, matured physically before anyone else and made the most handsome boy in class her boyfriend. Meda had no dad, only a mum. People in our village didn't paint her a promising life; but those people surely were glad not to have bet on that, because they would have lost the bet. The alpha boy in our class whom every girl had a crush on - I did too for a while but was very good at disguising it. For the most part I physically fought boys and even beat the lame ones.

Zaneta was a rotund, insecure girl who subjected those whom she felt she could put down to ridicule. She and Meda rejected me for not being girly enough to hang out with, Brigita and the less developed girls clung to me. Zaneta was the one who said that the mother-in-law of the parallel class teacher had deliberately cherry-picked the students, so they would give the teacher more expensive gifts. I do wonder from whom she heard that. For the first few years she acted like she and our alpha boy belonged to class A.

I was quick to catch the bait that my naughty classmates threw at me. Words that were intended to trigger a reaction from me: Chukchi, Japanese, Jackie Chan, Akira Maeda - called me to defend my reputation to prove that I was none of those things. They would use their two fingers to mock my Asian eyes and screamed in a weird manner to imitate the martial arts films.

The unsolicited attention came from the more senior students in the canteen, in the school hall, in the yard but not the library. These kinds of children bypassed the library like demons do with holy water, and it became the safest place to be. My taunters were usually boys. If any boy pestered me more than I could take, I'd tell Felix and he'd sort them out. But there were a few older girls who hissed and snarled the same names at me. There was no way my brother could have dealt with them, so I did my best to avoid them. They came from the surrounding villages and hung around until about three in the afternoon when their school bus took them home. By that time, Mama had her own lucrative coffin and funeral attire business. I prayed that Mama didn't send me up to the village centre to get some black thread and plastic flowers from the shops for her funeral wreath weaving. Whenever I had to go, my heartbeat so fast out of fear of encountering those girls. If I saw a group of students walking on the same side of the road, I'd cross over. 'Please ignore me, please don't notice me,' I kept repeating in my head. I felt ashamed to tell anyone about the older girls giving me grief, it was my personal burden that I had to bear. Why does it always have to be girls that make your life hard?

Chapter IX

I didn't know at the time that I was getting neglected at home. Nobody checked on my grades or my homework. Mama didn't attend the school meetings with my teacher - she didn't like any of the kids and their parents. My Mama's hands were swollen with infection from the spruce needles. She never used gloves to weave the wreaths. After her shop rebranded itself as a funeral needs store, Mama made all the right connections with the suppliers, and when she realised she could save on expenses by learning how to weave, our financial and social status got elevated once again. Her employer entrusted her with the entire business and eventually sold it to her. Mama officially became a businesswoman. People came on horse carts from neighbouring villages to buy a coffin at three in the morning. A preparation for All-Saints' Day or someone's death were the busiest times for her business. Someone's death was my Mama's gain. Both my sisters and even Mrs. Leach were harnessed into weaving wreaths to help meet the targets. We recycled old wreath frames from the cemetery waste bins. Felix brought the spruce twigs from the woods and my job was to make a few trips a day to buy reels of black thread and those tacky plastic flowers. The peculiar cult of honouring the dead in Lithuania has always been just a tiny bit ostentatious.

Come to think of it now, it was then that I frequently started drifting off and dwelling in the clouds. At school I couldn't focus, I didn't take heed of what my mother was telling me before she sent me shopping or tasking me with any other errands. Aware of the purpose of the plastic flowers, I came back with a bunch of them in different colours. I thought it was nicer and more interesting that way.

"Who sold you these flowers?" she asked.

"I don't know her name, the young one."

"Did you say it's for the funeral wreath?" What else would they be good for?

"No, but she asked me what colour I wanted, and I picked those ones."

"What was the issue?" I thought, "didn't they look lovely?" It was certainly not the reaction I had hoped for.

"You go back and exchange them now," that was an order.

"I am not going. Can't you go yourself?" I protested. Pointless.

"Go and exchange these flowers! What am I to do with them?!"

"I don't want to go! It's embarrassing!" I raised my peevish voice to retort. The exchange and refund policy were alien.

That's how we fell out with one of the shopkeepers: my siblings went to get this very trendy, big wall clock. They had sold out, but still took the money and supposedly placed an order for it. Our outraged mother sent the children to get the money back. The offended shop owner reluctantly refunded them and said he would never do business with our family ever again. They didn't like giving you a receipt either if you didn't ask for it, and sometimes gave back less change if you were a child who couldn't count. Like me. I have got better since though.

Agitated, Mrs. Luktuk came by, escaping her overbearing husband, Mama sent me to the shop to get them a bottle of cheap wine and a packet of the cheapest lollies for me. I walked turbo slowly. My Asian genes getting the best of me, Mama used to say.

"Walk faster, for God's sake!" mother encouraged me. "Did you not buy anything?" Back then, a child could walk into the store and say their mother asked them to buy a bottle of alcohol - yeah, no problem.

"Why no, I got sweets."

"Where is the wine?"

"Oh, no I didn't get you anything." Mrs. Luktuk said she was going to the shop herself.

My mother successfully ran her business, kept a whole household together and attended to our animals in the morning while we were at school. The afternoons and evenings were our shifts. Because of Felix's duodenum affliction, doctors recommended feeding him goat's milk. Mama bought Oleska, the most frightening creature with the longest and most twisted pair of horns ever.

But her two boys were the softest babies I've ever held in my arms. Their flesh was so warm and when they swallowed with their little baby throats, I felt it against my own neck, and I didn't want them to grow into horned, aggressive creatures like their mother. We had to get rid off them. Mama monetised them to pay back the local alkies for the jobs they did for us.

Looking after two cows, a goat, a pair of pigs and a flock of ducks took a lot of time and dedication. The milk had to be delivered to the creamery every morning as well, by bike, via icy roads in winter. It was a struggle that defeated me once. I pushed the piece of crap of a bike with two heavy buckets of milk, and when I reached my destination, the fear of descending the icy driveway made me turn back and go home. I told Mama that the creamery was closed, but it wasn't a legitimate reason because the lady who worked there always accepted late comers. Mama showed no mercy to me, but I deserved every blow - it taught me the value of respecting other peoples' hard work if I had none of my own.

The shop and household animals were vital sources of income for us, more so when Papa's precarious position in teaching became more apparent. Our mother's natural resourcefulness always exasperated our father but from that time onward, he became more peripheral to our lives. He couldn't hold on to any job for longer than a year. Come September he'd still be hanging around unemployed, and when it should have been him responding to the newspaper job adverts, Mama made telephone calls to schools arranging interviews for him. She'd put on her honeyed voice and extol the virtues of this overqualified, very experienced English teacher. There was a minuscule problem though - depending on the schooling direction you aspired to go in- he couldn't speak Lithuanian.

That September, Papka, like a hunger-struck wild animal, lurked around the house to the delight of our chauvinist neighbours downstairs.

"Hubbie has not yet found a job?" Papka always saw Mr. chauvinist as a benevolent acquaintance and failed to see the not-so-subtle ridicule. That mister from downstairs exploited the fragile relationship of my parents and put ridiculous ideas into Papka's head about hiring a solicitor to get a divorce, whereby half of everything we owned: a poky, twenty-five-square-meter flat, a couple of acres of land, the animals that he despised, my mum's shop and furniture obtained through the sweat of his children, would come into his possession. It annoyed Mama so much when Papka used the word "Ours" for everything.

One of those pieces of furniture was a corner sofa that Felix was constructing because Papka couldn't do it. While he was working on it, we received sad tidings - my sweet aunt had died. She had fallen down those steep stairs, sustained a concussion, refused to go to the hospital and two weeks later, her teenage boys had no mother.

Mama asked Jelena to take leave from university to accompany her. She took Varvara with her for the first time since she was a toddler and went to Kaliningrad. My brother and I were left in our father's care. My God his cooking was absolutely dreadful. Felix had to contribute in that department too. Mrs. chauvinist plaited my hair every morning. The cat, Vasily, didn't leave Mama's bed for two weeks and everyone desperately looked forward to her return home. On a lighter note, I learned a few Kazakh words and expressions, all about food, naturally.

My cousins were taken to St. Petersburg by their maternal grandparents and never saw their father again. After this heartbreaking event, my mother became more interested in religion and used that occasion to baptise my sisters, something she had longed to do for years. But no one felt a more excruciating pain than my uncle who started numbing it with alcohol. Perhaps, if he had stood his ground and hadn't let his children be taken away from him, he would have dealt with his loss better. My mama didn't think it was a good idea for the children to be separated from their father, but the state that my uncle was in meant he didn't feel capable of taking care of them. He comforted himself that the separation was temporary. Grandpa Alexey foresaw the future and entreated Mama to learn to drive. He vouched to fund her lessons and buy her a car if she did. It's astounding, it really is, how insular people can be when goaded by their envy and small-mindedness to sneer at anyone who tries to distinguish themselves from the crowd. Some of those people laughed at Mama for taking driving lessons at forty-four years old. They said even if she did pass her exams, where on earth would she scrape together the money for the car. And women, they were the worst. Not so many of them drove in villages then, so they frowned at my mother's masculine ambition.

"We don't need to drive, our husbands take us everywhere we need to go," they rationalised. The same women asked Mama for a lift when their husbands lost their license for drink-driving. The first car Mama owned was a white, spacious Nissan. The Leaches negotiated this purchase, and the settled price was paid entirely in single US dollar bills to the amusement of Mr. Leach watching the car seller count the bills.

"It's still money, isn't it, my friend?" he chortled.

Grandpa bought us a car. The following summer, Jelena went to work in Finland on the same farm and sent us money for the garage and other household expenses that we would not have been able to afford on our regular income. The Finnish farmer had grown fond of Jelena and her conscientious work, so he invited her back. Jelena's English was immaculate, which allowed her to do some translation work when the opportunity arose and make some pen friends from abroad. She surprised me one Christmas when I received a letter addressed to me from Santa Claus from Lapland. It was all in English. I kept asking Jelena or Papka to reread it to me over and over again. I'd pull out the letter to show it off to the other children.

"You see," I said "Santa knows me, he knows where I live and who I am. He sent me a letter". The letter became marked by finger marks from frequent touching. I used to bring it to school for everyone to see how cool, actually, how much cooler than them I was. I needed it, I loved the attention and status and it set me above most of my classmates and put me on a par with Zaneta and Meda.

They'd ask me to show them the letter time and again. I even pretended that I could read it. There was a myth going around that because my father was an English teacher, I could speak, read and write very well. I think I even convinced myself of that because no one ever challenged it.

Mama's business was still bringing in an income but there was competition in the village now, and the taxes she had to pay made it a little bit more difficult to sustain the profit. Nevertheless, she managed to squeeze all she could from it. She got a landline at home, which used the same number as the shop. To obtain that she had to go to the telecoms office in the district several times with bribes: fresh eggs, a fat duck, money, a big chunk of *salo* until finally the officers deigned to allow us to have a phone line installed in our flat.

Mum's customers would try to get through to her sometimes and I'd pick up the phone at home. They'd ask me to hang up and not to answer until Mama picked it up in the shop. Only three of my classmates had phones at home.

"What's your number, I'll call you today after school," Zaneta proposed. We called each other often just to be able to use the phone. The excitement we derived from turning the numbers of the round dial and listening to the line to connect. "What are you doing?"

"Nothing. You?"

"Same."

"All right, you call me tomorrow!"

"Okay, I will!"

"Bye!"

"Bye!" It felt great to have someone to call you. It made you feel a little bit important.

With the gradual improvement of your life grounded on your merits comes a great envy - even from your own spouse. Driving to big cities through busy roads unnerved

Mama, so she mainly drove to the district centre, some forty kilometers away, to nearby towns and Kaliningrad. The trips to Kaliningrad were very long but fun. We used to wait in the long queues at the border, often arriving late at night and wake Baba Toma up. If the queues were enormous, Mama would start saying politically incorrect things aloud.

"Lithuania is free, Lithuania is independent! Why the hell do you dignified citizens of the independent state keep crawling to the Tyrant Russia for cheap petrol and cigarettes?" Some people's jobs were to cross the border a few times a day with as much petrol, cigarettes, vodka and Russian over-the-counter medical supplies, as the travel regulations allowed, to resell for slightly more but for lower rates than they charged in the shops.

Felix quickly picked up driving and Mama trusted him to take over on the road, praying there would be no police patrol on duty. Our father showed no interest in learning but was extravagantly free with insults towards Mama. Whenever he was in the car, he'd start criticizing her for allegedly being a bad driver.

Mama said it was pure envy. One time she had had enough and almost drove into a lorry, which freaked him out so much, that it triggered his radiculitis pain.

It was then that I developed an intense fear of and fascination with ghosts. Varvara told me that the night of our aunt's funeral, she couldn't sleep and had witnessed our aunt float in through the window in the dress she was buried in. To me ghosts were real, and I was so affected by such stories that I had to sleep with my head covered with my duvet, only just leaving a tiny gap for air. I lay like that for hours, sweating and holding my bladder in. The creaks of the dry piano at night added to my anxiety. I shared Varvara's experience with Mama, who took offence and assured me that ghosts didn't exist.

"Only Varvara could come up with nonsense like that. If ghosts existed, how come not one of them has ever come to see me?" she opined. "At least for one split second, my loved ones would show themselves to me."

My brother played on my fear by telling me that one of the previous residents had hanged himself in the basement. I said I was never, ever going down to the basement. I imagined what it would be like to be locked up for a night in there. There had always been so many things I was afraid of: Mama dying, encountering a ghost, being accosted by a dog, stupid children, getting stabbed by Oleska, riding the swings and the wind blowing in my face. Greta Leach had a swing that she would sometimes let other girls swing on. Some had no fear of going really high up in the air, but I felt terrified, and once my fear was apparent, they pushed me more vigorously while my heart dropped to my heels and needles paralysed my feet.

Chapter X

In 1998, Britney released her debut hit and drove many teenage girls around the world mad, but I would only discover her tantalizing, baby-voiced songs years later. Before the clock struck twelve - signifying the beginning of that year, we were perching around the kitchen table, enjoying a tranquil and harmonious dinner. The family picture felt complete. I was waiting for the stocking outside our flat door to be filled with presents, mostly for me, not just from Mama, but from Jelena too. New Year preceded Orthodox Christmas and was a big deal for us, hence I enjoyed two occasions for presents, on a good year - three. Being the youngest in the family only feels good when you're a child.

We had managed to squeeze ourselves around the tiny kitchen table when Papka enthusiastically rolled in through the door two hours before midnight, with his black fedora hat and coat covered in snow. Mama's face clouded with disappointment. She and Jelena began exchanging mutual whispers of arcane comments that the two shared when they wanted the third one in the room to feel unwelcome. The rest of us just knew that there was only one side here that needed to be picked. Feigning animosity towards Papka didn't stand the test of the emergence of the gifts from his green sports bag. Varvara received a camera that she had requested beforehand.

Mama shook her head in disapproval and Jelena hissed vivid adjectives meant to provoke remorse and guilt in Varvara. The camera was not a cheap purchase, and it was a thrill that could have been foregone. Papka was a gullible customer - a delight to rogue sellers, who were rife in the questionable back corners of public transport stations. A gullible and awkward customer who felt comfortable in such places. This extravagant gift soon broke. Without a consumer guarantee it was an utter 'throwing money to the wind' buy. Jelena got a thick fashion magazine that was more like a catalogue of the things that she was unable to afford. Even if she could have, she wouldn't have spent her money on those. Papka loved Varvara the most, Jelena the least, didn't know how to talk to Felix, and I was still the youngest and cutest one. How does a parent of many children distribute his love? Well, it's not an easy task for sure.

Both of our parents used to say to us that if they cut any finger of their hand, it would hurt equally. Mama said that Papka was just repeating her words.

When Jelena was only five, Papka hit her with his briefcase because she couldn't read in English. The buckle of the briefcase injured her head. She never forgave him for this unsolicited bout of violence. That and many other things: the tears and embarrassment of the agonising experience at the passport issue office, a childhood plagued with peer racial abuse, self-abasement and poverty.

No one was safe from Papka's explosive brutality.

I had to ring the Leaches to get Mama one day because Papka was repeatedly punching Varvara's back with his fists. He had been helping with her homework and when she kept failing to understand the exercise, he lashed out.

Varvara was crying, but he kept hitting her again and again. I hugged my knees silently behind her, why, I thought was he punching her in the back so pitilessly, wasn't she his favourite?

"Mummy is bad, daddy is a saint. Isn't he Varvara?" Mama shamed my sister, but Varvara didn't admit that she was wrong about our father, didn't tell mother that she had been right all along and change her loyalties. "Mummy is bad, daddy is a saint?" she said this several times, in front of our next-door neighbour who was there in the capacity of a witness and kept shaking her head. Papka sat in the armchair, saying nothing as he was accustomed to doing if someone else was present. Varvara said nothing too, just sobbed.

On the night of New Year's Eve, Mama prepared a plate for father at the table and ordered everyone to remove themselves from the kitchen to her bedroom. We scattered around her and watched TV. Besides Mama and Jelena, the rest of us were happy with Papka's presence and tried not to think of what the remaining visit would bring. At least we knew he'd be gone in a few days' time and the household dynamics would go back to normal. No more shouting and swearing, no more physical altercations between anyone, no involvement of neighbours, no gossiping, no theatrical performance from anyone. But even the usual scenario of the usual fight between mother and father didn't follow the usual course of events one time. Just that one time, something extraordinary happened that puzzled me greatly. Nothing like it had ever happened before and never did after.

Papka never aimed at Mama's face, nor did he that time when he hit her somewhere else, causing her to fall on the ground.

Could it have been shock that caused him to run away and sleep in a hay barn for a few nights? I can't tell. Would he have done it if it had been winter? The atmosphere at home was that of the elephant in the room. If it was shame that made him flee, then hunger overrides all our noble emotions, developed by the primitive people when they had had enough to eat. After a couple of days of no show, he began sneaking in for a quick lunch that Varvara kept for him behind our mother's back. My moral instinct told me it wasn't right that she was feeding him while Mama wasn't at home, but I couldn't be angry with him either - he was funny when he came in, he joked and made me laugh. We both laughed so much that Varvara called me a retard which only made me laugh more.

Eventually Mama discovered him in the kitchen on one of those afternoons, but she didn't make a scene. She passed him as if nothing had happened, which he took as a sign that it was okay for him to come back home and just like that, life went on again.

Another turbulent summer ensued. "Young children don't let you sleep; adult children don't let you live" Mama used to remark. "Have pity on your mother" she tried to appeal to our ungrateful souls and when it fell on deaf ears, she'd say; "Why did I bear that many children? Not one of them is worth bringing into this world. The second they're out, squeeze them hard between your legs." Such a drama queen. Nothing she ever said hurt my feelings - when you hear it so many times, you just don't hear it anymore.

Varvara had a new boyfriend from a neighbouring village, introduced by her new best friend with whom she spent every weekend. Her friend had a separate room, and her mother allowed her to hang posters on the walls, play loud music, invite friends for a party, wear make-up, go out and have her boyfriend stay at night. They even watched Titanic together and sobbed when Jack died. This friend had a big bosom, and she was nice to me. She was much friendlier than the one from the city. I stayed with them one night and I loved how those two adorned my face with make-up and took pictures of me posing in front of a giant poster, I thought I had never looked prettier in my life. A paedophile's wet dream. The little bit of attention I received from that friend shot me up to previously untested levels of boisterous energy. I acted like a rabid dog until I literally panted my heart out. This new friend was way less subtle in her dress taste. She had to wear every trinket she owned all at once, but everyone back then thought it was very cool. She was really nice. She even helped us to re-decorate our wallpaper once and she was always polite, and she shared her clothes with Varvara. She even introduced her mother, who was a teacher, to our Mama. Mama didn't like that new friend. She thought the girl was promiscuous and that her mother condoned her illicit behaviour and the friendship would have dire consequences for her own daughter.

Varvara tried to kill herself because Mama didn't let her go out when she had already made plans with her friends that she would. She wrote a suicidal letter to her new friend in which she called Mama a bitch and said that the only person who understood her was her big-bosomed friend. Mother found that letter. Now here is the thing, Mama usually had a low opinion of people who committed suicide or attempted to commit suicide for an empty cause like unrequited love or being misunderstood by the world, unless a person was suffering from severe depression, like she was. But the latter cases solely related to mature adults who had lived and suffered. There was a family in our village in which two women attempted suicide and one woman succeeded in committing suicide - all because their lives had been impacted by Oxycontin. Pointedly, Mama said that people in that family didn't play with the full deck of cards. 'Not everyone was at home' as the saying in Lithuanian goes. When my sister took all my mother's sedatives, the affair was handled domestically so as not to spark gossip. Not even I was exposed to a view of it, which was a good thing knowing what a blabbermouth I was. Absurdly, Varvara poisoned herself again. She mistakenly took a sip of a brown liquid in a *Coca - Cola* bottle in the fridge - a cow's medicine. One of the cows was ill so Mama kept its medication in a plastic Cola bottle in a 'cold place out of everyone's reach'. Cows have bigger organs; their medicine doses are much stronger than humans'. We did without an ambulance. A local nurse from the GP came over and washed-out Varvara's stomach.

"I will make you drink all the water in the well if I have to, but I'm not calling you an ambulance!" Mama was angry. The benevolent nurse promised Mama that no one would find out about this incident and she kept her promise. She was a mother of four herself and had two daughters the same age as my sisters. Although it was unintentional this time, still, how could Varvara be so dim and take a sip of something that looked just like Coke, from a plastic bottle that had a Cola label on it? They never bought us products like that at home - ever - so why would she, for one second, consider imagine it was Coca - Cola?

Totally inexplicable.

We never had any contact with our paternal relatives, but there has definitely been some irascible genes passed down from at least one side of the family tree. The devil got into me and made me tear up one of Mama's pictures and throw it in some metal cylinder behind our house. I decided that I didn't love her anymore and this was my way of convincing myself that she meant nothing to me anymore, but I was not capable of not loving Mama anymore. Her threats to take her own life because she was so fed up with it still elicit tears and a sense of my own life ending. In one of her overly dramatic episodes, she told us that she had taken all her Relanium to pass away in her sleep, then she pushed up a sofa-bed to block the door from inside and went to bed.

My siblings were less credulous, but my terror set off such a torrent of cries, that Jelena broke the glass of the new bedroom door to rescue Mama and cut her hand as she did so. Her blood was dripping heavily, I was startled. Mama jumped out of bed, pushed the sofa-bed back off the door and slapped Jelena for breaking the glass. She didn't seem to be bothered about dying any longer.

"You fool, what have you done?! Look what you have done! What were you thinking? How am I going to afford a new glass now?" Mother was furious. She slapped Jelena. Felix had to get this guy who had been in prison for murder to measure and put in the new stained glass for us. Poor Jelena. It was my fault. She sent me to the pharmacy to get her some bandages and antiseptic, and she cried silently. I got her the wrong thing at first because I was too embarrassed to explain to the pharmacist that her hand was bleeding. All I said was that I needed something for an aching hand, so she sold me some gel. Jelena looked at it and said it wasn't going to be much help and asked me to exchange it for something else. The second time, with all the confidence I could summon up and without much elaboration, I told the pharmacist that her hand had been cut deeply by glass. My childish brain was paranoid that if I gave out more details, they would ask more questions and then the people in the queue would find out the whole story and they would spread rumours in the village. Besides, the old pharmacist couldn't be trusted - all day at work she maintained the undisturbed flow of gossip passing through her. The hand healed quickly but the effect imprinted on my brain didn't. My mother openly threatening suicide signaled to me that I could get attention from her in the same way. I screamed when I couldn't get something, and when I was ignored, I said I was going to hang myself. I took my skipping rope and went to her bedroom. I didn't know how to tie a knot, so I just crossed and pulled both ends of the rope at my throat as much as my strength allowed. I don't think I was even going to choke myself in such a way, but that was enough for my family to rush into the room and take pity on me. Mama covered her mouth with her hands when she saw me, and she said nothing. She pressed my crying face to her chest and stroked my head. No one said anything. They must have been flabbergasted.

Chapter XI

Here I was, a graduate from Year One of primary school, continuing to take out the books from the library, and reading the simplified versions of the world's classics like "Little Women", "A Christmas Carol", "Charlie and the Chocolate Factory", then returning them on time. Now Brigita could also take some books out, but the librarians didn't want to give them to her, because she'd return them damaged and pervaded with her household smell. I was fine being friends with her in summer, her dirty appearance didn't put me off, even though it was strange for me when she asked me to plait her hair and it felt so oily. She'd come to mine every day to ask me to go out. I couldn't always get away from my chores, so she'd tag along with me. I always had some errands to run before I could disappear outside for hours. Mama opened the door once and said I wasn't home, but I was in the toilet and when I heard her say that I yelled loudly.

"Mama, I am at home, tell her to wait outside, I'm in the toilet right now!" Mama lied to Brigita, but I sabotaged her.

"Nastassja can't come out with you right now, she has to weed out the vegetable garden." On another occasion she challenged my persistent friend.

"That's okay, I will wait for her," Brigita responded.

"Don't you have to weed out your garden, Brigita? Your family does grow vegetables?" Mama knew that Brigita's folks were incapable of growing their own food or keeping animal stock - they were unbelievably lazy. If they sewed some seeds or planted potatoes in spring, nothing would grow because they didn't tend to the fields in summer. If someone gave them a calf or a goat out of pity, the wretched animal would end up looking like a washboard because it was underfed.

"It's too hot to work in the garden at this hour," she said, "We don't weed our garden when it's that torrid."

"Fair enough. You should do it very early in the morning or when it cools down", mother said. "Then go home and mop the floor."

"We have already done it" Brigita said.

One late morning I went to theirs and her brothers were all disheveled and still in their beds. Mama never allowed us to sleep that long, not even on the weekends. She used to say that having children is one thing, but to teach them to work is quite another.

Brigita's mother was a slattern, her excuse was she was blind. Not entirely, but severely visually impaired. Both her parents apparently were. That was why they got a massive chunk of benefits every month.

"Why work if you can get free money?" people pondered. Sometimes, Brigita's father ordered everyone to clean, wash the windows and floors, he also made a lamp shade from lighters of different colours, and stuck half the kitchen wall with cigarette packets. Even if he was tidier than his wife, he was still pretty useless and didn't like working. He drank and dressed as a woman on several occasions. He'd go shopping for large-sized bras in the market and say they were for his wife. The woman was tiny, so they definitely were not for her. Ironically, Brigita's father had good taste too. He'd paint his nails neatly, wear a wig and proper make-up, high heels, and lingerie, had jewelry on - he couldn't help it! When he was not going through these funny periods, there was nothing feminine about him. Before his cross-dressing inclinations made Brigita and her siblings the object of virulent abuse, while the dirty little secret was confined to the domain of their household, some man, on the request of his missus, brought them some pancakes.

Brigita's father opened the door clad in his wife's clothes. The man was baffled. He asked why he was dressed as a woman.

"My wife washed all my clothes, so I had to put on one of her dresses, don't mind me," was the answer. While the pancake dish was being swapped for one of their own, the visitor felt he was being duped and said:

"Well, my wife washes my clothes too, but I don't walk around in one of her garments." He went home with his empty dish, and this is how the cat was let out of the bag.

It would have been better for my friend if her father had really just had no clothes to wear at that time. So much did children pay for the idiosyncrasies, misdemeanours, or the origin of their parents, that I wonder if the parents ever sat down with them and talked about how none of that would matter once they finished school and got out of the village. Ugly ducklings would turn into swans, fat kids would become slim, people would judge them by the content of their character wherever they went and not by whose children they were, and that there was a chance for them to grow up a little bit messed up. I knew once I left school and became a famous singer and actress, every little demon of a child that had made me shrink in size when I passed them in the streets or school halls, would see my face on TV and regret calling me those silly names. They would realise that they didn't like me because I was better than them. By this time, I was sure of who I was going to be when I grew up, and not becoming that was not an option. Brigita had the same dream, but I was sure I was definitely going to make it. We gave each other a promise that whichever of us made it first in show business, she would invite the other one over.

I loved the theme song to Titanic so much that I made Papka write the lyrics down phonetically for me, and without learning what they meant, I memorised the whole song by heart. First my classmates, soon the entire school knew me as the girl who sang the 'Titanic song'. I was so terribly shy to sing it in front of the crowd for the first time that I only agreed to do so with my head in a cupboard and my back turned to the children behind me. What can I say, I was becoming popular, and I loved cupboards. However, my first proper gig happened at my primary school graduation party, where I sang the same song in Russian and I didn't expect either of my parents to show up, but Papka did. His presence embarrassed me. I was instantly on the alert that somebody would make fun of him and ruin my moment. His eyes were entirely and proudly on me, but I felt anxious for his sake and my own. Dear papa, forgive me please that I was always so ashamed of you. I opened my mouth, and I poured my heart into the song, because I could at least understand half of what I was singing about. I also received a medal for being the best singer in the class. Mama dismissed it and told me she'd rather I had received a medal for maths or something. The head-shaking neighbour, also a maths teacher, shook her head in agreement. She was a good woman, but she loved gaslighting me sometimes.

Varvara paved a path for me at school with her performance of the Titanic song, stealing the hearts of the teachers and students. She did a catwalk show once where the teachers went up on the stage after and said:

"We know that there is a special girl among us here today who will definitely go places." Mama now had at least two daughters going places.

I loved performing and hadn't had stage fright after my debut in a cupboard. I felt validated. Way before Brigita and I became friends, Evie and Princess talked me into throwing a little show for my neighbours, in exchange for sweets. The idea was a success, my esteemed neighbours paid us in the currency we asked for, gathered outside our house, and enjoyed our creative performance. They clapped for us and praised us. I wanted Mama to come to see me perform too, but she always frowned on such things. She didn't approve of either of her daughters taking part in entertainment activities. She was especially worried about Varvara's grades. Mama was adamant that all her children would go to university, whether they were adept at studying or not. With Jelena doing well in the academic field, Mama had no lesser plans for Varvara, even though she didn't have such ambitions. It was only in her last year at school that she exerted a little bit more effort to achieve higher grades. She did okay in the end. She continued her friendship with her big-bosomed friend. Her new boyfriend had left her for another girl, but she took him back to have her own revenge on him just so she could dump him herself. Mama understood very well that there was no chance of her second daughter getting in on free or partially paid conditions, but where was she going to get the money to pay for it? It didn't matter, she would have to get the money from somewhere. Varvara was going to go to university, preferably to the same one where her older sister studied. She would keep her in check and encourage her to study harder that way. They would manage. They would have to. Really thick students went to universities, just because their parents had the means to pay for them. We were no worse than them.

    As for me, I was on my high horse that summer when I scribbled a poison pen letter to Laura and left it at her door. At some time before that, I had watched a film where a blackmailer sent a letter in cut out letters and I thought that was genius. My replica was a very poorly executed version of it - I wrote it, I didn't cut the letters out of magazines. it would have taken me all summer to do that, and I needed it right then. In my letter I wanted Laura to know that she was not a good friend. She was a thief and a two-faced girl and I hated her. Also, that her parents were alcoholics, which made her the daughter of alcoholics. Laura's father knocked on my door and sneakily asked to see one of my exercise books. I was astonished that he had traced the letter to me so soon. Terrified and cowed into complying with his demand, I was going to look for one of my exercise books, when Mama rushed to me and commanded the impertinent man to leave that very minute. They got into a row and Mama deliberately raised her voice in the hall for all the neighbours to know that she was being harassed by him. The plan worked. Some neighbours came out and took Mama's side, embarrassing Laura's father, who fled the house swearing. The heaviness of my action started setting in and I suddenly felt guilty and filthy that I had implicated Mama and that she had yelled and belittled Laura's father. Mama came back inside and discreetly, because you know the walls were thin and we had loud voices, closed the balcony door, and asked;

"Did you write that letter?" I was quiet. I thought if I remained quiet, she would stop interrogating me and leave. "You must tell me if you wrote that letter. You know he can call the police for that, and we'll both be in trouble." Oh no, no, no, no. "I will not punish you if you did write that letter, for there must be a reason why you've done it." I wasn't used to being spoken to like that.

"Yes," I uttered.

"You did write Laura that letter?"

"Aye." She didn't beat me or ground me.

She started a smear campaign against Laura's father to send him the message that if he tried something against us, he would not succeed because he was the one who had come to our house and tried to harass me, a minor.

Mama had the whole neighborhood on her side.

I did get my comeuppance twice as harsh and Mama was powerless to protect me, just like Laura's father was powerless to get justice for his daughter, when a bigger dog was involved in the crime. But this would happen a little bit later in time.

Laura was not a nice nor a sincere friend, more like a serpent in the garden of Eden, in my garden, as a matter of fact.

The downstairs neighbour, whom my cat disliked so much for reasons known solely to him, had a granddaughter staying with her in the summer, but the dainty, precious thing was kept away from me and the rest of the local children. You can only imagine what sort of things she was told about us lot, judging by her conceited demeanor whenever she was in sight. Her grandparents had attached a hammock for her outside their windows which looked tantalizingly inviting. I could see the girl lying in there serenely under the two tall pine trees on which the thing was secured, with her drowsy grandfather reading nearby. People said that this man was one of the last descendants of an ancient and prominent Polish-Lithuanian noble family. I have to say, there was something odd about him. One day, I witnessed the whole household leave in their car permitting me to try the hammock out, as I had never lain in one before. I thought it was sensational. It was better than lying on the ground or any other surface I'd ever wallowed on before. That great feeling when you have access to something that is not yours without the proprietor being aware of it, and the frisson of excitement overtaking you when you know you might get caught. Maybe not many people get to experience that. Maybe it's just me, the cheeky, infernal child. I had only bragged to Laura about it, just to show how resourceful I was.

"Nastassja, Laura told us that you have been lying in our granddaughter's hammock when we're not at home", my posh neighbours confronted me unawares.

"Me?" I said, "I don't do that."

"I hope you're not lying, Nastassja, because the hammock is our granddaughter's, not yours." How petty, how base. How much lower can these sententious people stoop, but they did. The last time I laid my provincial, shabby rump in that delightful thing, they found me only five minutes after their car had driven off.

"You...get out of my granddaughter's hammock. Get out!" The disgust in that woman's face made me feel like I was the wretched and undesirable heroine in the first half of the Mexican soap opera season. Later they discovered that she was indeed an heiress and the long-lost daughter of the rich family. She falls in love with her brother, who actually was not her brother, but an adopted son whose real family was actually the one that raised the heroine. The babies had got mixed up in the hospital.

I could feel my face being engulfed with crimson shame and without spluttering a sound, I rose to my feet and walked off. This awkward moment truly did make me feel like I belonged to a lower caste. Somehow, every other stupid situation that I had been in with the other children in my yard and at school, was wiped out by the abhorrence in my neighbour's face. I could now imagine the things she was saying about me to her granddaughter. But nothing frightened me more than my mother's wrath. At the time I felt lucky that this woman hadn't told her anything, although you never knew with Mama, she might have surprised us all.

But what happened next really opened my pretty, hazel eyes to the murky realms of injustice. Impeccable

Rasa and I were messing around our community centre's newly tiled ramp porch. We were so hyped up, that things got out of hand. Rasa picked up a heavy stone and flung it on the stairs, which broke the freshly--laid tiles. Although not being very life savvy, my common sense told me we should abandon the newly discovered playground before anyone noticed the damage. Little Rasa refused to go, she liked it there and failed to grasp the apprehension I harboured. I lived there, she didn't. I'd be questioned, not her, I understood that much. But then again, I reasoned, she was the culprit; if she liked breaking those tiles, what did it have to do with me? My conscience was clear, and I shouldn't feel bad about it. My library was in that building and I frequented it weekly. Everyone working there knew me. I felt safe past that door. I felt respect and peace in that place.

A caretaker came over for her shift and was utterly appalled at what she saw. She yelled at us and ordered us to go home. The next thing I knew, my entire house was buzzing with noise, the raised tones of several women were combining to bring me out to the staircase and make me confess to breaking the new tiles outside the community centre. I came out and said I hadn't done it.

"Rasa, you broke those tiles, why don't you tell them?" And I raised my voice too because everyone else had. My little friend was being sheltered inside their home by her aunt and uncle, who spoke on her behalf. Angry faces, pursed lips, and scornful looks. I looked at Mrs. Chauvinist's face and I hoped it would mellow, smile, and put an end to this charade, but she just stuck to her script. And who wouldn't? Mama would have done the same, but I was a child and believed that all adults were fair, especially teachers. Feeling like the worst person in the world, I slumped on the floor by the door and sobbed my heart out. Jelena was the only person at home. She was whiling time away in the kitchen and asked me what had happened.

"I didn't do it! I didn't break those tiles, but everyone said I did, but I didn't!"

"Who said that?" She was calm and didn't even bother coming up to me.

"Everyone! Ona! She accused me but I didn't do anything!" The second I spouted that out, Ona dashed through the same door suspiciously fast as if she had been standing outside and waiting for a cue. She talked to Jelena briefly in a suspiciously calm tone and left.

Perhaps Rasa's relatives feared that they might need to pay for the broken tiles and her conduct would have made them look bad anyway. And here I was, a scapegoat. I didn't even know if Mama believed me, everyone just continued rubbing it in that I was a very bad girl and should be ashamed of myself, that I was big enough not to act like that and when was I going to grow up. Shame on me. This commotion even reached our village mayor whom The Chauvinists so eagerly were trying to befriend even before this incident. In the end, no one had to pay for anything, the matter settled itself. It's just that I was made to feel like I was on probation or something and I didn't hang out with Rasa again.

Summer went by. Drawing close to the middle of August when the water is too cold to swim in, and we are on the cusp of a change in season, most young souls like me began itching for the advent of the new school year. We got excited about the clothes we were bought specially for September the first; the new tracksuit and trainers for the physical education lessons, only to be worn for the first few times to show off and then maybe replacing your usual school outfit towards the end of the year. Girls looked for every opportunity to miss PE lessons. It's good for the parents when the child grows slowly, but the child always wants new things. I wore the same teal fancy tracksuit for a succession of years - the pragmatism of buying two sizes bigger clothes. Mama dressed me in a white shirt and a denim pinafore dress, Jelena waved my hair. An effortlessly obtained summer tan added to other students' curiosity to gawk at me.

My second year in primary school proved to be more challenging, mainly because I didn't find maths interesting and allowed my attention to drift away. Instead, I engaged in pranks with the boys and heard my name called out by our lovely teacher when I was being too loud. Because I lost the thread of the subject, I became afraid of it and mentally disassociated from it. Felix did all my maths homework, but in tests I barely passed. My writing stopped evolving too, I simply didn't follow the grammar rules, while reading remained my strongest point. Mama didn't go to the parent's meetings with my teacher, she came to us - living in the teacher's house had advantages. She told Mama that I had a very short attention span and when I was bored, I picked up a pen and started fiddling with it. Other than that, she said I was capable of learning.

Mrs. Chauvinist gave me a few Lithuanian language lessons, despite her previous remarks to Mama referring to my siblings.

"Dear, your children's writing in Lithuanian has many mistakes", the kind of response she expected was not the one she was given.

"My children go to Lithuanian school, you're a teacher, you teach them how to write without mistakes."

After a careful assessment, Mrs. Chauvinist deduced that my main hindrance to spelling the words correctly was not hearing them properly. Well, how could I hear the notes then if I couldn't hear the words?! This impelled me to pay more attention to the grammar rules to prove that I was not deaf, but purely and simply ignorant of the complexities of the Lithuanian language declension rules. At no point in my life, did I feel hindered by my multilingual upbringing, but teachers at school often liked to patronise me a little, and the only time I didn't mind it was when they said they would add a few extra points to my score due to my supposed struggle.

Chapter XII

Our relationship with the chauvinist family downstairs resembled the karmic partnership often spoken of by the astrologers: you don't want to associate with them, they get on your nerves, they push your buttons, you passionately dislike them, but you often feel drawn to them and feel that the universe deliberately puts you in situations together to learn the karmic lessons. Of course, it's all just a load of nonsense because it is just what being neighbours sometimes is.

The pipe in the basement burst and flooded the whole level. Neighbours were bailing the water out. Everyone was on edge. No one from our family was pulling their weight in this effort: Mama lay ill in bed, Papka and Jelena were away, I was eight years old, Varvara was looking after Mama and Felix was tending to the animals and running the usual, perpetual smallholder errands. The disgruntled neighbours demanded someone from our family go to the basement to help.

Suffering from a high temperature, Mama rose from bed, cursed the neighbours, got dressed and descended to the underground. The very same day she was taken to the hospital in an ambulance. Mama was diagnosed with pneumonia and asthma.

The chauvinists had a son who carried the torch for Varvara. He was the kind of person who didn't know how to say no to people and wore his heart on his sleeve. When Mama was in hospital, he drove us in his father's car to visit her. He was the only young male that Mama trusted Varvara to go out with and she wouldn't have minded having him for a son-in-law, but my sister, like most foolish young women, didn't find herself attracted to kind, shy and sensible men. She could only be his friend and nothing more. But like most young women who can only be friends with these men, she knew perfectly well how attracted those men were to them and ostensibly innocently exploited their friendship. In the young women's defense, those men were very foolish to think that a woman would take them out of the friend's zone and extend their offer to something more intimate.

Everyone in our family liked this boy. I found him very funny and teased him for how pale his skin was. One summer, he helped us to harvest the hay without disclosing his hay fever; that's how much he liked Varvara. His parents sometimes teased her by calling her their daughter-in-law, but that was a sarcastic gesture because we all knew this would be a problem to them.

It's sad how political ideologies drive a wedge between common people, who think that their opinions are more significant than they really are to those making the decisions influencing the way common people live their lives. This boy's father couldn't help engaging in political debates with our mother. At every given opportunity he hankered to prove to her how great, how much greater his country was than hers. She, on the other hand, never felt like she had to contend.

"Our country was once so vast; the horses of our Grand Dukes drank water from the Black Sea."

"Horses don't drink sea water", she was pithy. Apparently, they can drink sea water if they're desperate, but it's better if they don't.

"We are the nation of many great poets and writers," it is not untrue, but what he probably was referring to, was the world eminence of those authors.

"Oh yeah," mother said, "Like who?" she bent her fingers to count the next set of names. "We have Tolstoy, Dostoevsky, Chekhov, Pushkin. Who do you have?" On my mother's account, Mr. Chauvinist took a while to come up with the name.

"Oscaras Milasius".

"Let's be poor but fair. You mean Oscar Milosz? Anyway, he was of Jewish descent." She made her point clear. Speaking of poverty, our neighbour regularly rubbed Mama's face in it that her people were abysmally poor and that the quality of life in Lithuanian villages was far superior. Mama retorted that there was no shame in being poor, but it was a shame to be cheap, "Like a cheap neighbour, for instance", she said.

These sorts of conversations would come up time and again over the course of years. Mama said once that if he continued poking the bear, she would remind him of that time when he came beseeching her to travel to his homeland in Samogitia, to wash his dead mother's body for the funeral. There was not a single soul in the village willing to perform this service for them, except for the local alcoholic woman if they paid her.

"You should have seen the house he grew up in, and he is mocking the poverty of the Russian peasants", she shook her head and cursed in Russian and said, "We couldn't take the clothes off his mother's dead bod., I had to use scissors to remove them. It's amazing how quickly people forget these things." Mother never reminded Mr. Chauvinist of that time.

The practical aspects of death seemed natural to my mother.

"Fear the living, not the dead," she used to say. Mama sold coffins and washed and dressed dead humans for their last physical appearance in public. She was the person whom people rushed to in the middle of the night when their loved one had passed away, and no one else told such lurid accounts of unfortunate events as my mother.

Neighbours. Hate them or tolerate them - you must live with them.

Long before I was born, there lived an arts teacher downstairs. She had a talented son, whom she sent off to study music in the city. The son began raising a glass after his every performance and before he knew it, the glass took hold of him. The son moved back to his mother, relying on her for full support.

People asked his mother why he didn't get a job.

"My son's hands are for playing music and not for manual labour", she defended him to the day she died.

The son continued to live happily as a fortunate loser. The pipes in his flats were burst for ten years and when he carried his bucket out to empty in the outdoor public toilet, we locked our doors to prevent the smell from emanating through the keyholes. Mama used to say that if Papka lived on his own, he would also carry his bucket out like that, and his pipes would be broken too. This once promising musician neighbour of ours didn't care much for music either, but to mark the historical significance of our village, the mayor commissioned him to paint the coat of arms. As a last resource, he pinged a few instrument strings at the community centre events. The only difference between our neighbour and other village drunkards was his beret and a scarf he wore when he went to a pub. Stupefied, he would fiddle with his door key for ages, addressing it and swearing at it for not obeying his inebriate orders to open.

In my early teenage years, I was uncomfortable to encounter him alone, particularly after that time when he spoke about women's breasts to me when mine were just beginning to poke through my blouse. It was probably why he spoke like that. But when I was still a little fiend, my friends and I would take turns to ring his doorbell before swiftly whizzing off chuckling - it was the best fun. I couldn't help feeling sheepish whenever I passed him in the hall afterward, but I told myself that there was no way he knew I was one of the hooligans. I soon found out that this man's cousin was a respected thespian who hailed from an even smaller village in the neighborhood. This piqued my interest, so I sat on the bench outside our house, just to catch a glimpse of her clearing out the debris from one of the collapsed walls in his flat.

Hunched and gracefully lithe, she pushed the wheelbarrow laden with heavy bricks with all her senior might, a humble face farrowed with intellect and signs of torture from every role expressed through the years -far different from my neighbour's gratuitously smug face, which was not seen clearing his own mess that day or at any other time. His cousin paid for everything: she had given a promise to his dying mother to never abandon him, which she kept until she drew her own last breath - thus leaving him comfortably homed in one of those old people's institutions which he would never have been able to afford.

As I sat on that bench watching her pushing the cart, I longed for her to find me interesting and worthy of conversation. I wanted to tell her that I was also going to be an actress when I grew up. I imagined her being impressed with me and honoured too that I had chosen her profession. I expected some sort of anointing from her for being the next important actress in our country's cinematography to come from a small village. The place with nothing special about it, nothing at all to suggest that great and important people hailed from there.

Chapter XIII

Two thirds of the students at my school were getting free meals. For many this was the only food they put in their mouths. One girl fainted out of hunger and when told to go home to recuperate, she chose to stay.

"There is no bread nor other food at home", she explained.

They fed us fairly and deliciously: a bowl of soup which most skipped, but Mama dinned into me that "You must eat soup at least once a week to prevent your intestines from drying up"; something I could be telling my own children one day. The main course usually consisted of meat or fish, and a small dessert that we could sneak out of the canteen. Zaneta paid for her food and sneered at our unappreciatively full cheeks munching away. The boys in my class challenged the teacher to say why Zaneta wasn't getting a free meal like the rest of us.

"So what that her parents own a lot of land, it's not like she can eat it." We all looked at the teacher to give us the answer to this valid question.

Every morning, we collected our meal cards with our names from the caretaker's desk by the cloakroom. Minutes before the lunch bell rang, we vied for the best spot by the door to extricate ourselves from the room and ran as fast as we could to the canteen. Brigita fought harder than anyone else for her spot by the door, which she frequently held. Boys kicked her hard with their feet, leaving the boot prints on her clothes. If we succeeded in imploring the teacher to let us leave earlier to get there before the other children, we never stuck to our promise to walk there quietly. Boys teased us that Brigita stuck her fingers into our drinks to put us off having them. Nobody wanted to sit with her and if anyone did, they ceremoniously whizzed away from that child screaming "They sat with her, they stink just like her now!"

In the class, we sat in pairs, but some had no desk partners - I didn't want to associate with my summer play mate at school. I joined the club in deriding her and poking fun when I could. But that was only when we were with others. After the lessons concluded and everyone went home, we'd stay behind in the room and play teachers or shop assistants. I tried to tell Brigita to tidy up her desk, but she just didn't know what order and harmony meant. I showed her how to arrange her textbooks and how to preserve her books for the students for next year by swathing them in a plastic sleeve or a cover made with wallpaper. She said she didn't have any wallpaper at home. Unlike Brigita, I derived a lot of pleasure from putting things back in their place in our classroom at the end of the day. There was a set of cupboards and drawers stuffed with books, toys, and a varied bunch of trifles at our disposal between the lessons. We were well provided with most things, except the convenience of toilets. The newly refurbished indoor bathroom was violated by older girls, who must have got confused about its use, as there cannot be any other logical explanation why they would rip the panels off the doors, break locks, smoke inside and not flush after themselves. Thanks to their ghastly behaviour, we were forced to run out in the freezing cold winter, with no coats on - the cloakroom ladies refused to give our coats out until all the lessons had finished to stop us from slinking away early. You might have called the outdoor toilet French, but there was nothing French about it. It was awfully dirty, with nothing else in it but a few holes in the ground and a horrible compound of cigarettes and faeces. The stench stuck on you after each visit. But one time I was grateful I could use it as an excuse for my own untimely expulsion of my bodily contents. When you're a child engrossed in playing, you sometimes abandon your physical urges, like the need to eat or use the bathroom in time. I joined Meda and other girls in the game we were playing after my trip to the toilet.

"What is that smell? Smells like poop," Meda said pointedly.

"It's probably me," I said, "I went to the outdoor toilet," that sufficed to explain the smell. No one had a reason not to believe me. If it was Brigita, it would have been a different conclusion to the same story.

Children were not the only ones repelled by Brigita. Mother deigned to grace us with her attendance at an event. She brought food, as custom dictated. Every parent brought something, but no one touched it until the formal part had finished, and the teacher invited us to the table. I had learned my lines and looked forward to reciting them in front of the parents, but Brigita began nibbling at the food.

"Brigita, we're not eating yet. Please wait until we finish the event," the teacher whispered but everyone pricked up their ears.

"Teacher, please, I really, really want this ham. If I don't eat it now, I think I will faint," she said in the most plaintive cry she could master.

"All right Brigita, you can have some now," What else should the teacher have done?

Mama grabbed my hand and stormed out of the room. She never attended my school events again until she got called in because I had got inside the cupboard and refused to come out. That's what they told her at first. What I told her when she arrived was that my classmates had ganged up on me, forced me into the cupboard and fat Zaneta held the door with her flesh mass precluding my escape from the cupboard. Mama was incensed. What she must have imagined was her worst nightmare - her baby had been racially attacked and bullied. Whether I got in there myself or was forced into it, I was looking for safety.

Mama's impulsive high-pitched yelling at my classmates was cordially extinguished by my teacher.

"But why, Nastassja climbed into the cupboard of her own accord in a fit of pique, because she wasn't awarded the certificate of merit."

It wasn't as simple as that! I felt I deserved the certificate of merit together with Zaneta, Meda, and the alpha boy - the only three students in our class to be acknowledged for their above average grades at the end of the year. I fully expected to hear my name called out by the school headmaster amid the throng of teachers and pupils. This pipe dream was a testament of how removed I was from the real state of my grades, or maybe I just believed that they would still give the certificate to me because of who I was. But perhaps who I thought I was, was only the case in my own personal world where I won everything. In objective reality, nobody thought I was special and deserved the merit based on criteria other than my academic performance. Oh, the indignation made me morose, so morose that I was itching for an altercation with those who got their awards that day, but I couldn't hold my own, so I sought refuge in the cupboard. They thought it was funny and held the door from outside until our teacher came back and stopped the commotion. That felt cathartic and I immediately assumed the role of the victim - if I couldn't get the recognition for my efforts then I at least would get the sympathy for a scratched ego. I wanted to see my classmates punished for ganging up on me, but only because I allowed them to. I was supercilious, and I acted like a man's genital.

Mama was lost for words when she heard what had really happened, which compelled her to calm herself and navigate out of the situation as diplomatically as possible. She did it so well that by the end of the school day, I was playing with my assailants like nothing had happened and she was genially chatting to my teacher about another topic.

Chapter XIV

The school year was wrapped up, the summer ensued, harbingering the long-anticipated home improvement works executed by Felix, managed by Mama and largely funded by Jelena, who was working in Finland again.

Something new was in my oldest sister's life - she had a boyfriend now. My second oldest sister graduated from school but not without the threat of drama.

The predatory music teacher tagged along to the end-of-year events, under the pretext of being the chief coordinator of such things, with Varvara endorsed as one of the only two solo singers in her tier. She was of age now too, which must in his eyes have made his intentions legal and unequivocal towards getting her. He belonged to the group of men who married early because his girlfriend had got pregnant - that's how it used to be done back in those days. Today, she would be his baby Mama. He always felt deprived of his freedom to explore other options. In his not so old but not so young years, he looked at young girls hoping that some of them might find him handsome and grant him access to carnal pleasures and more. Rumours arose that there was something going on between my sister and the music teacher. The aggravated wife followed him to the students' only outdoor get-together, looking to wrench the hair of the girl who had seduced her husband. This type of husband liked to talk about his wife in a pitiful way to win the sympathy of those young, attractive girls. The episodes of passionate jealousy from the wife only helped to illustrate the 'I told you she was crazy' point. My sister's scalp was safely preserved from the hands of our music teacher's wife, but our mother's nerves could not escape from the tongues of the small town.

During the kitchen renovation, Mama made quite a few trips to a hardware store for building supplies. We had to buy them in small amounts because there was never enough money for bulk purchase. The wooden panel walls were the trendiest thing at the time and everyone copied each other. A la style de Nordic - although no one could tell how this trend came about. On her way home Mama picked up Mr. Luktuk, who flagrantly asked her if it was true that Varvara was shagging her music teacher.

Mama abruptly hit the brakes and I can imagine, in her most authoritative manner, told him to get out of the car. He laughed it off and probably said something like "Come on", which only exacerbated her to use her native tongue swear words, which compelled him to leave the car.

Varvara's hair was damaged by poorly executed hair bleaching at home that summer. Yes, she got that yellow-blond tone. That lovely boy who fancied her bought her a pack of blond hair dye after she got accepted at the University of Agriculture, solely on paid terms which he also kindly covered until granddad gave us the money to reimburse the costs. Now my own sister looked like a fox. First, Mama walked by her without noticing, then Jelena walked by shooting suspicious looks, lastly Felix asked her if she had changed her hair colour a little bit.

The neighbours teased my sister, Mr. Chauvinist called her ginger. Mama's nerves couldn't take it anymore and she told him she would make his son take Varvara to a professional salon to reverse the damage. The dramatic shift in colour highly complemented her exotic looks.

In our village, one only had to be careful not to earn a lifetime nickname, by which your legacy would be permanently sealed, superseding your posterity. There was a harmless, old gentleman with a long gray beard, a bachelor if you like - a weighty curse to any man who didn't care much for the delights of a married life. He was happy hoarding all sorts of what he thought to be vintage junk. I never knew that man's real name, he was forever remembered as Buddha. Some people didn't do anything to deserve a nickname, it was either their last name or their appearance. Another man in the village was enough on the larger side to raise associations with a loaf of white bread. They nicknamed him Loaf. His doughy genes passed to his two sons, who were in turn nicknamed Little Loaves. To be fair, he was a bit of a philanderer, a gossip and mean to my Mama once, so I feel he deserved every nickname in the world. He would abandon his wife for a bit, then each time he came back she was pregnant again.

Cars were a rarity in those days. Mr. Loaf and one of the other parents drove Jelena and other girls to music school on an alternating basis. Mama didn't always offer the money for the petrol costs, so one late evening, Mr. Loaf barged into our home and accused Mama of freeloading. He asked her how much longer they were going to give her daughter free rides. Mama handed him the last cash in the house, with which he bought alcohol for his friends. The next day, the other parent came in to apologize and said that Mr. Loaf had acted entirely independently and that he never minded driving Jelena to the music school.

Another man moved from the bigger town and insisted on demonstrating the previously unheard-of Kung-Fu skills to the local labourers at work. It is needless to say what generations of the village residents called that man for the rest of his life, even on his deathbed. You will have guessed what his sons would have been known as.

My dear brother Felix, on the other hand, carved himself out a reputation as a conscientious and dexterous home improvement man. When he had completed embellishing the walls of our kitchen with those wooden panels, he was invited to do the same in the short-lived, unlicensed, but highly scandalous nightclub in our village. It was the first and only night club we had. The club opened up later that summer and brought so much joy to the youth, and those who we would still consider young today - people like me - but past their prime back then. No, I'm joking; fewer than a few people over thirty would set foot in the teenage meat market, where girls danced in a circle guarding their handbags in the middle of the floor, and the boys pushed the walls with their backs, waiting for that beer to kick in to maybe then ask one of the girls for a dance. Where groups of virile lads arrived in cars with unknown number plates from neighbouring towns and villages to provoke a fight with our locals. The bravado was greatly encouraged and welcomed by our boys. Was my brother involved in any of the scraps? He never came home with bruises or scratches. Except this one time when he jumped out of a tree and landed on his back on glass splinters. Felix enjoyed entertaining girls, and this was one of his show-off episodes.

The sight of his bleeding back scared me, but he emphatically threatened to hurt me if I told Mama. For two nights he slept on his old, ragged T-shirt to prevent staining the bed sheet until our next-door neighbour asked Mama if Felix's back was healing well. The way he enquired about it was done in a typically patronising manner: he couldn't imply enough how inane my brother was for doing such an utterly silly thing, which was hurtful for his parent. If it was not meant to be delivered as a direct attack on her parenting, it was always taken that way. For whatever reason, Mama scolded me for not telling her, but she really had no idea how menacing her only begotten son could be. If it had been Varvara who had entreated me not to tell, I would have blabbered about it in a heartbeat. Mama loved us all equally, but Felix's life was worth more, naturally! When he was born, she said she felt as if she had given birth to not one, but many sons.

Felix was a bit of a heartthrob too.

The women in our household could all agree how sorry we felt for a girl who used to visit her grandmother during summers: a nice, quiet girl, blond. They went out for a few weeks in summer before Felix broke up with her; considering how short summers are, the dalliance must have lasted a wink. Arms locked with her girlfriend, she'd roam around our house, wearing a checked blazer - how bizarre, girls don't wear clothes like that - only old men do, I used to think. She called our home once, Mama picked up the phone. "The girl was polite, and you could tell by the way she talked that she was a city girl," said in Mama's own words.

Village girls were largely obtuse and cultivated their masculine behaviour to put down other girls, thinking that was what would get them noticed and respected by the boys. There were exceptions, of course, but in my early puberty, I was not that exception for I didn't know any better either. Maybe city girls matured quicker and were advanced in their knowledge of the laws of dynamics. She asked Mama to pass her festive wishes to my brother. Very sweet, Mama said to us, why Felix couldn't be with her she couldn't understand. Mother indirectly asked this question in front of him in the presence of other people, as if not asking him but she wanted him to understand that she was. This girl ended up marrying the boy from Greta's house who first pined for her sister. He had an exotic complexion like Felix, so he was the type. Marriage is a strong one as far as we know. Like all men, Felix regretted ghosting her when it was too late, because on several occasions he mocked that marriage, but he should have expressed his judgment to someone who cared.

Chapter XV

Mama used to say that a man (a human being) plans but the Almighty laughs at his plans.

Mama planned to squeeze in a short three-night trip to Kaliningrad before the school year started. For hours we languidly and in an almost stationary fashion queued at the border in our white Nissan, listening to the indefatigable voice of the Russian radio presenter. I sprawled on the back seat munching food I was not usually allowed to eat at home. Mama felt this reprieved her from cooking, but otherwise tainted her dutiful maternal obligations. I felt ecstatic thinking of cans of condensed milk and tins of sardines in tomato sauce. I knew that grandpa would give us money and Mama would spoil me with some new clothes. Mama was always so much more pleasant when she had money.

Only in Kaliningrad did I savour the most delicious pastries, chocolates, biscuits, and tins of condensed milk. I loved the taste of white Russian bread. Mama scolded my brother and me for not showing more restraint in our appetite on each visit. Felix was a growing lad, but I was just greedy.

"People will think I don't feed you!" she reproached. She also often used to remind me to chew my food before I swallowed it.

A sweet tooth ran in the family. When Felix was a child, he swirled tiny holes in cans of condensed milk and sucked them empty, leaving Mama's cake baking intentions unfulfilled. The whole lot of them!

Grandpa Alexey only drank his tea if half of the can was poured in it to fuel his mental sharpness. He kept a bunch of biscuits and chocolates by his bedside. When I asked him why he kept them, he said, "The night is long." Papka shoplifted cans of some saccharine beverage before they caught him. He didn't steal them for his children, as one might imagine. He also stole honey. And thick English dictionaries from bookshops.

"How does she manage to keep her voice so tireless and upbeat?" my mother said of the radio presenter. "Nastassja, can't you eat like a normal child? Look at the mess of crumbs you have made! Please, don't gorge yourself on the biscuits. Have you really finished the whole packet?" I really had. "You will get sulfur burps again." This was the same woman who boasted that when I was a toddler, my thighs rubbed against each other. "You always had a great appetite" she used to say. A doctor asked her why she fed me that much when I was one year old and had pneumonia. Mama answered faintly that she wanted me to be healthy.

Both my brother and I hankered to see our youthful uncle. When we arrived, Felix went to crash at his place despite Mama's efforts at dissuasion - he stood his ground firmly. By this time, my uncle drank and got taken advantage of, as usually happens, by a group of users with whom you'd never ever socialise if you weren't at a very low point in your life. They cling onto you like an unwanted man who doesn't give up if you're a woman - it's rarely a man whom a woman wants to be wooed by - it's usually the one who persists until she convinces herself that she's attracted to him. Those people smell your vulnerability and begin pursuing your company because they know you're too good to pass. They know you'd never ever even look their way normally, but right now is their chance to fawn on you because your judgment is poor. And now you're weak, inebriated, and abused by them. They no longer rub their hands together when they drink at your expense. You paid for everything with that set of china that you sold to keep the party going - now you want them out of your life and your home, but you cannot get rid of them.

We stayed with Baba Toma as always. I didn't enjoy watching afternoon TV. 'Why can't I be in the kitchen listening to the adult conversation?', I wondered. Mother was against any child gawking at the faces of the grown-ups when they're gossiping about the members of their community, not that it ever stopped me from overhearing things I was not meant to. My uncle wore a denim suit and paid no attention to me when I slunk through the kitchen about eleven times to use the bathroom. I wanted his attention. I wanted him to talk to me, to ask me questions about my life, I was his youngest niece. Why did nobody take me seriously, I was nine years old, that's almost ten! That's almost primary school finished. Not quite though, I was going to begin my penultimate year of primary school - year three. I was developing quickly and was the second tallest girl in my class.

That night I was awoken by an excruciating tummy ache. Mama gave me some digestion calming drops, but I still ached still until an early hour of the morning when the pain subsided and I had a shallow dream. My appetite for breakfast wasn't present, but Baba Toma boiled me some eggs and I loved semi-hard-boiled warm eggs with a pinch of salt, toast with butter so I had a little bit, but immediately threw up. Mama had no time for real concern: we had to pick up our uncle and grandfather on the way to the town on an agenda of official appointments. I remember how warm the day was. I gazed out of the car window, outside this run-down government building, waiting for Mama to sort her paperwork out. Suddenly a pang of nausea got the better of me. I excused myself to grandpa and uncle, who were with me in the car. The compassionate look my grandpa gave me unnerved me. It was some kind of reproach from him I expected, but not kindness. I can't remember if I expelled anything, lurking at the side of the building, people passing, going in and out of that building made me feel very self- conscious. I was ready for someone to shame me for vomiting in a public place any minute now. Guilt crept inside me, and I wanted my Mama, so I walked into the building. There were mainly middle-aged women, looking older than their years, queuing up for the little registration windows. There was no Mama in sight.

Before anyone cared to say anything unpleasant to me, I returned to the car. How I wanted Mama to come back and show me sympathy. She came back shortly and decided that on the way back, we should pop in to see another relative of ours and see some medical person for a prescription.

The visit to some walk-in health office was brief. They prescribed a maroon liquid for me to drink three times a day. The old German cobbled roads jolted every fibre in my stomach. There was not much Felix could do about that other than to drive more slowly. Bless him, he didn't answer back when several times I told him his driving was hurting me.

Our relative had this black cat that lay on my stomach when I rested on a couch while the adults were catching up in the kitchen. She lived in a spacious flat with a very tall ceiling. Mama used to say that in this flat you could cycle, that's how spacious she thought it was. Felix stayed with me in the room and talked to me gently like only an older brother can. The maroon liquid induced frequent bouts of nausea, but each time I ran to the bathroom, hardly anything came out. We were going back home the following day; Mama told the relative that she'd go back to the same medic again to ask for a sick note for me to skip the queue at the border. The thought of queuing up for hours evoked a horror in her face.

Mama and Felix dropped me at Baba Toma's and drove off for their last errand - it had been a very long day for Mama. Maybe the absence of my usual boisterous spirit prompted Baba Toma to look at me with such a concerned eye. She asked me if I wanted to lie down. I said I did. She put a cushion under my head and covered me with a throw. She asked me if my stomach still ached, I said it didn't anymore. She asked me if I was hungry, I said I wasn't. Then I asked her if I was ugly. Baba Toma asked me why on earth I thought that, well of course I wasn't ugly. I told her that I knew I wasn't pretty, but I so wanted to be pretty. She told me not to worry my head with such nonsense, I would grow up to be a beautiful girl. I fell asleep but I didn't believe her.

Chapter XVI

On the morning of the following day, we were bidding farewell to Baba Toma, and I could not walk with my back straight anymore. I was clutching my stomach with both hands, the maroon liquid made no difference. As Mama intended, we returned to the same healthcare office to ask for the sick note for the border officers.

"I just need to cross the border and then I'll take her to our local doctors if she's still unwell," Mama said, but the medical practitioner referred me to see someone more experienced, who would run some tests on me first. Mama's countenance yielded to sharp anxiety.

"We are not allowed to exceed our three-day stay; we have no visas."

The woman said she couldn't be responsible if anything happened to me, so it would be better if we drove back to the town we had been to the day before to see her colleague. She would make a phone call. Off, we drove via the same cobble road again. Just like the woman had told us, they took my blood. The sample of urine caused me excruciating bladder pain and I couldn't pass a stool.

"Your child's results are not good," the lady said.

"If only you could give me the official document to bypass the queue at the border..." Mama's face was warped with the mounting stress which made her voice high-pitched, powered by excessive oestrogen levels in a tense situation. I can talk because I am the same now. "The thing is, we only came on a short visit on a visa-free entry. We cannot stay another night; we must be on the other side by midnight. We have no health insurance here; we don't live here…"

"Woman!" The patience of civil servants is always short. "You're not taking that child anywhere tonight! The doctor will examine her first thing in the morning and then we'll know what to do with her. Come back tomorrow. I'll issue you a note for the immigration office to extend your stay."

They put me up in a children's ward with orphans. I had never encountered children from an orphanage before. Mostly, those children had simply been abandoned by their alcoholic parents and had had their heads shaved to prevent the spread of lice among them. Papka had bought me a brown-haired doll that cried if you pulled the pacifier out of her mouth. The state of happiness and excitement of not going home yet and staying somewhere different mixed with the apprehension of Mama and Felix not staying with me. There was a red-light hotel sign just outside the hospital window, which reminded me of films I had watched about New York.

"Look Felix, a hotel," I said. "Tell Mama there is a hotel just outside the hospital, she probably doesn't know it. You don't need to drive back to Baba Toma's." Felix said nothing. "How I'd like to stay in a hotel. How good it'd be for all of us to stay in a hotel for at least one night. Actually, if they decide to keep me longer in here, you can stay just right there in that hotel." My mind went to the possibilities of what sort of rooms they had, what colour carpets and curtains. Were they red like their sign? Was it just like in the films? Soon after Mama and brother left, the nurse came in with an enema which she used on me for the purpose this thing was designed to be used – to give you tremendous discomfort and wonder if it's really necessary. At least she was nice to me and asked if I wanted tea with biscuits. I wanted it but it never arrived. Slowly but noticeably my strength began to drain away. Those kids curiously approached my bed and asked what my name was. It was not me they were interested in, but my doll. I didn't want to let go of it as I was scared they wouldn't give her back to me, but I couldn't say no, so they took her to their room to play with. The entire time I felt on edge hearing them romping next door, hoping they wouldn't damage or lose her. "If they don't return the doll to me very soon," I thought, "I will tell the nurses." The good children brought back my darling in one piece.

I believed I was going to get better by breakfast, so when the time came, I pulled all my strength together and got out of bed. I couldn't straighten my back and every step required a lot of effort but motivated by the bowl of porridge and those biscuits I had never got the previous night, I shuffled down the corridor, looking for the kitchen. When I found it, I was told that the doctors had told them not to feed me yet. My determination not to miss my meal entitlement was driven more by the Pavlovian response evolved in queues in the school canteen, than any real hunger. I then wanted to use the bathroom, but on my way there I realised that I didn't feel strong enough to make it, so I dragged my feet back to the ward. The young and pleasant doctor came to look at me. He pressed my tummy in a few places, asked me if it hurt, how much it hurt and ordered another enema. I spent another night in the ward, the children came up to me again asking to play with my doll, oh, how I hated to part with her. Luckily, a nurse came in and told them to leave me alone. They were good kids and did as they were told; the peremptory tone of address must have been familiar to them.

When Mama and Felix arrived the next day, the young and pleasant doctor told them that he was actually a gynecologist, but he was certain that there was a problem with my intestines. He wanted me to be seen by an experienced doctor with an irascible temper in another hospital wing. I couldn't walk so Felix carried me through endless corridors, passing through countless doors. On our way, we encountered a bitter, older nurse who shamed me for being big enough and not walking on my own two legs. It was unusual for Mama not to say anything to such remarks.

This wing appeared to be more welcoming in ambiance. Patients were relaxing in front of a colour TV when we walked in and some of them smiled at me. There were no other children or young people among them. I was seen right away by the infamously cantankerous doctor, who I thought was very affable. My examination took about five minutes. He called Mama in after and said that my appendix had burst three days before, which had caused peritonitis and he was going to operate on me in one hour's time.

Chapter XVII

A funny, fat, one dimensional black man wakes up during his operation, looks down at the open cavity in his midriff and dies.

Corny nineties Hollywood comedies left me with this indelible impression in my mind, which now seemed very plausible. This surgery was meant to stop me from being sick, but how scared I was to suddenly wake up and feel the pain or witness my own blood and what not. The life I knew: long, warm summer days in my village, our river, Rubik tethered to his kennel under our kitchen window, dragging his chain and moving his steel, beat-up bowl, Vaska forever shedding fur and ceaseless trips in and out of the flat, our teacher-neighbours, my sisters, my library, my school, my lovely teacher, even the rascal boys who teased me, our cows and pigs, the detestable goat, Oleska - everything that meant my life to me was softly beckoning me to come back soon. The concept of death was entirely removed from me, still I was afraid of the rest. In a hospital ward of several women, Mama sat beside me as we waited for the nurses to collect me. I didn't want to part with my Mama. I asked her if I could say Hail Mary in Lithuanian, one of the prayers learned from Religious Studies at school. The silent faces of the women looked curiously at us. I said the prayer sincerely, feeling its every word and I felt calm. I couldn't help wondering if Mama was proud that I knew it and she didn't - a pinch of vanity had to find its place even at solemn times like that! Mama was unusually tranquil and mute. At last they came, with a gurney just like in films, carefully moved me over onto it and wheeled me out. Mama and I held hands as she walked along. The young nurses smiled. I'd noticed that all of them had their ears pierced with different gold earrings and couldn't unnotice that afterwards. Whenever I looked at a nurse, my gaze went to her ears at once. I kept asking Mama when she would pierce my ears. She had pierced Varvara's ears, a few other girls' and even one boy's single ear. Two pierced ears could land you in a lot of trouble if you were a boy, but one ear was cool. Those who had not yet had a pair of gold earrings bought for them wore a cotton thread until it healed, or borrowed a pair of hypoallergenic earrings which we simply called 'medical earrings.' My Mama didn't have any medical background, but she had a tool kit with needles and syringes and a Chinese cupping set. I could vaguely recall her placing them on Varvara's back to help with the cough. The sight of her red, swollen back freaked me out. Mama said she had lent the cups to someone, and they had never returned them. Often Mama reminded us how she managed to feed her children when there was no money for food while administering injections to people for a fee.

She said that she had had many different jobs in her life without any qualifications to do them, because she had common sense, like her father, my beloved granddad Alexey. In kindergarten, Mama oversaw meal plans, thoroughly calculating the portions and calories for kids, and put together menus, because no one else could. She played the piano and curated music and performance activities, and again, no one else could do it. But Mama's stories always came to the same conclusion; she had no paper to prove that she could do her job. What she meant was she held no official certificates, so when the daughter in-law of a superintendent, a recent college graduate, showed up at work, Mama had to step down from her role. She didn't mind being eventually relegated to a laundry assistant's job, as long as she had a job, she used to say. Some of those daughters-in-law were so thick, Mama said, that they really struggled to understand the handover and relied on Mama to continually teach them how to do their new jobs. It didn't matter though; they were university graduates, so they were right for the job.

We met Felix in a corridor, his face was serious. And just like in hospital dramas that I used to watch at home, the swinging door opened in front of me, and this is where we parted. I looked back before the door blocked the view and saw my tall, dark, handsome brother holding my shriveling, young mother in his arms. They wheeled me to the operating theater. The cantankerous doctor was all dressed up. I was helped to move over to the operating bed, my body felt infirm. I was told to lie on my right side, pull my knees to my chest.

There was another woman in the room, and she had a nice pair of earrings with red stones. She seemed angry to me. I was looking at the tiled wall in front of me when I felt a needle stab into my backbone and almost instantly I felt drowsy, my eyelids heavy, the senses blunt and voices muffled. I thought I heard the angry woman say:

"They brought her in for surgery, but her neck is dirty." I lay on my back, I felt someone run their finger horizontally over my stomach. The tiles, the woman's earrings, my dirty neck.

My granddad Alexey sold his shares in an oil company which could have been worth significantly more in the future. He had intended to pay for the tombstone for my sweet aunt, but then I got ill.

"The dead can wait." he said, "We must save the living."

When I opened my eyes, I was relieved that the surgery only seemed like a wink and that I hadn't woken up before they stitched me up. The first thing I heard was some man named Kutchin screaming in the next room and the nurses screaming back at him for urinating himself again and for being a pain in the butt. I was very thirsty. It didn't take them long to acknowledge my awakening. A long-bearded doctor, who checked me, allowed me a few drops of water and I couldn't stop telling everyone how kind he was. Everyone else said he wasn't, and some patients complained about him being hard-hearted. There were two tubes inserted on each side of my lower abdomen that protruded like alien antennas. I had a drip in my arm, a tube in my nostril, a urinal catheter and another tube wrapping me across my back to distribute the anaesthetic to my gut.

The next day, Tatjana Nikolajevna came to introduce herself as my soon-to-be Godmother. She had that youthful and attractive appeal of a young woman who was mature enough to exert her authority over you, but not strict like your mum.

Young girls feel drawn to that energy. Tatjana Nikolaevna let me squeeze her hand as hard as I needed to when one of my antenna tubes was being removed from my stomach. The other one stayed in for a bit longer. Twice I endured the agony that in this day and age could have been foregone. Jelena rang me, I was brought a telephone receiver to my bed only to make myself teary, reminded of the sadness of being abandoned. I asked her how our cat, Vaska, and dog, Rubik, were doing. Some very ill woman was brought in and placed behind the curtains and then removed the next day. She died.

I had to learn how to walk again.

Spending so much time lying on my back made my head too heavy to carry on my shoulders. Since my surgery, Mama always said that I had a strong guardian angel. Three days later, I was moved to Tatjana Nikolajevna's department where several young nurses with pierced ears fussed around me. Two weeks later, I was baptised in the hospital ward. When the priest told me to denounce the devil and spit on the floor, I was so nervous because I didn't understand what he said, so I knelt and kissed the floor. Everyone laughed, I looked at Mama who spat a few times to demonstrate what I should do. I did what she did and denounced the evil entity. They had forgotten to bring me a pair of knickers, so each time I knelt I was conscious that everyone could see my bottom, but apparently no one noticed anything. I wore Greta Leach's white Christening dress that was way too short for me now, but at last I got to wear one. Jelena came with her boyfriend, but she was not allowed to visit me, so she just dropped off the dress and a few other things for me, among them a picture of Rasa and I hugging my beloved mongrel, Rubik. In the picture, I wore socks and worn-out summer wedges, trying to fit it with my little friend's outfit. The priest hung a cross on my neck, which I used to scratch the long, healing scar on my belly. How elevated I felt for having my Christening certificate. I clutched it and kept it by my bedside before Mama said she'd keep it safe for me. After the stitches were removed entirely, I was concerned that I would never be able to have a stomach like Britney, but the nurses assured me that in no time I would be able to participate in a beauty pageant.

I was not allowed to eat any solid food, which was very difficult when my bed faced the hospital canteen counter. Now I knew how our stupid dog felt when it salivated at the sight of people eating. At night I dreamt of *kugelis* with sour cream and begged Mama to bake and bring me some.

"What is that thing she keeps asking for?" someone asked Mama.

"*Kugelis*, oh, it's nothing. It's just a potato pudding." Mama sheepishly dismissed it. "You know, she's a country child." She said this and hoped that people understood where she was coming from.

Embarrassment aside, the doctor told my Mama if I wasn't a healthy country child, raised on organic potatoes and fresh air, It was very likely that I would not have survived.

"Number four! Number four you haven't collected your food!" a woman's voice from the canteen yelled.

"Here! I'm here! I haven't collected it!" I raised my arm to attract her attention.

"It's not you, Nastassja. You're not eating yet," said Mama. How displeased I was with her for only bringing me a teddy bear, a towel, a bottle of mineral water and a camera when she came to see me for the first time.

"Where is the food?" I asked.

"Not allowed."

For one night, she was allowed to sleep next to me. It was the best feeling in the world to have my Mama with me. I had so much love for everyone and felt love around me and I had never felt happier in my life. I was the only child in the whole department and enjoyed every minute of kindness, laughter, the chlorine disinfectant smell, the food smell, the attention and the *Muneca Brava* telenovela from Argentina. The delight of this new, exciting discovery with the beautiful protagonist I could claim as mine when I'd tell Brigita about these series. "Oh, she'll put her thumb to her lips again when I tell her that. She will lower her eyes in envy. She's me, the beautiful brunette is me and Brigita will not be able to say anything to that!"

Felix came to visit me too, he was pseudo-flirting with the young nurses and asked me which one of them I thought was the prettiest one. I overheard Mama telling someone that he and this girl, an unbelievably distant relative to us, had been to the Zoo together but decided they couldn't be a couple because they were related.

Towards the end of my recovery, I became cheeky and pissed a few people off. I told this woman I thought she looked like a man. She said I should wear a turban then because my father was a Muslim. To the kind, long-bearded doctor I said that I would come to his funeral, but he didn't laugh, no one laughed. He never came around again and never brought me another chocolate.

My Godfather was Tatjana Nikolaevna's brother and he had the sweetest young boy. The kind of boy you would want to kiss and carry in your arms, and protect and listen to his cute, childish voice forever. Maybe he was five years old, not older. Pure innocence. I liked to slap his hands for no reason and when he complained to his mother about me, she disbelieved him. I am so ashamed of how I treated that boy; I don't know why I was sometimes so cruel. Please forgive me, Slava. It is unknown to me how and where you are now, but to me, you will always be that adorable, little, blond boy with feeble, little hands. I wish I had never done what I did to you.

When I finally got discharged and could run again, Slava, Tatjana Nikolajevna's son, and I used to race to the shop to get a Rum baba – the tastiest thing I had ever put in my insatiable gob until that day. They were nice, well-brought up boys.

I was happy to be alive.

I wouldn't have been if it hadn't been for my mother's love, grandpa Alexey and God. God awakened me twice, and He gave me the strongest guardian angel to watch over me. So many people had a part to play in saving me, most of whom I was and will never be able to thank.

My washed-out intestine needed to grow back its bacteria culture; the doctors ordered Mama to buy me yogurts but there was no money for that. Baba Toma made home-made kefir for me instead. Every drop of her cow's milk went into my entrails. My Godmother didn't know she had a distant, extended family on her father's side until the day of my operation. Nor did the people who allowed Mama to sleep on their couch and Felix on the floor by her side in their living room. We were utterly broke. Grandpa said Mama was dressed like Chairman Mao. He gave her money to buy herself new clothes.

Back home, Papka had no job again but overbearing Ona entreated the school headmaster to give him a job on account of my unfortunate illness. Varvara went to University with Jelena. My sisters did a wonderful job cleaning and preparing the home for our arrival. It was spotless.

Felix got baptised a few years later. He was a big lad but was terrified of the priest, so Mama had to make these arrangements for him. My father said I should not have trawled through the garbage bins with Brigita - that is why I got ill. He had nothing more to say about that.

On the day of my hospital discharge, Felix took a picture of me in front of the red-bricked building, then a petrol station and finally with the statue of Lenin. In each one of those pictures, I had my arms spread in the air. I posed in many pictures like that until the day Varvara told me it was distasteful to do so. I love my family. Love saves lives.

Printed in Great Britain
by Amazon

56274984R00089